Arthur James Weise

History of Round Lake

Saratoga County, N.Y.

Arthur James Weise

History of Round Lake
Saratoga County, N.Y.

ISBN/EAN: 9783337193102

Printed in Europe, USA, Canada, Australia, Japan

Cover: Foto ©ninafisch / pixelio.de

More available books at **www.hansebooks.com**

ROUND

ROUND LAKE PASSENGER STATION.

HISTORY

OF

ROUND LAKE,

SARATOGA COUNTY,

N. Y.

BY

ARTHUR JAMES WEISE, M.A.,

AUTHOR OF THE

History of the City of Troy, N. Y.; Discoveries of America to the year 1525; History of the City of Albany, N. Y.; Troy and its Vicinity.

Entered, according to Act of Congress, in the year 1887, by
ARTHUR JAMES WEISE,
in the Office of the Librarian of Congress, at Washington.

PRESS OF
DOUGLAS TAYLOR,
BOOK, JOB AND CATALOGUE PRINTER,
89 NASSAU STREET,
Corner Fulton, New York.

PREFACE.

As shown in the initial pages of this work, the French were the first explorers of the vast forest-clad region between the Mohawk and St. Lawrence rivers. The name, Saintonge, given it by Samuel de Champlain, in 1609, has, as I believe, been corrupted by mispronunciation into that of Saratoga. The so-called Indian name, Kayarossos, designating a part of its territory, is also derived from the French.

The information presented on the succeeding pages was obtained with considerable painstaking, particularly the numerous names which appear in the foot-notes. The publication of the work has been approved and sanctioned by the Round Lake Association.

It is a great pleasure to me to mention and acknowledge the generous courtesies of the Rev. William Griffin, D.D., the Rev. Joseph E. King, D.D., and the Rev. H. C. Farrar, D.D., and the helpful favors of Joseph Hillman, and the kind offices of John D. Rogers.

ARTHUR JAMES WEISE.

TROY, N. Y., August 8th, 1887.

HOTEL WENTWORTH.

ROUND LAKE.

The scenery of the valley of the Upper Hudson between Troy and Saratoga is bordered easterly by the distant range of the Green Mountains and a wide foreground of undulating hills. Westerly a continuity of high land limits the view of the open country beyond. The landscape along the river dispreads itself in brooky meadows, arable fields, and short stretches of woodland. As far as Mechanicville, the Rensselaer and Saratoga Railroad runs between the Champlain Canal and the Hudson. North of the village, the road, by a reverse curve like the letter S, bends westwardly around the south side of Round Lake, and passing the station extends northwesterly to Ballston Spa.

Round Lake, three miles in circumference, is picturesquely environed by gently sloping hills, woody knolls, and grassy meadows. Long Lake, four miles westward, disembogues by an outlet into Round Lake, which discharges its water through Anthony's Kill into the Hudson, seven miles eastward.

The grounds of the Round Lake Association, about two hundred acres of land, lying west of the lake, are in the town of Malta, in Saratoga County, New York, nineteen miles from Troy, seven from Mechanicville, six from Ballston Spa, and thirteen from Saratoga Springs. The highway on the east side of the grounds runs through Maltaville, a mile northeast of them, and through Jonesville, three miles southwestward.

The sun-flecked depths of the cottage-clustered wood are entered by broad avenues diverging from the gateways at the passenger station on the east side of the railroad. Narrow lawns brightly bedded with flowers border these approaches and the paths extending from them. Beyond the prettily-built summer homes along the west side of the majestic grove appear others of varied architecture embowered by the branches of the tall trees surrounding them. In the central part of this sylvan retreat is a large pavilion with thousands of sittings for the people attending the religious meetings, summer schools, Sunday school assemblies, lectures, oratorios, exhibitions, and concerts held there in the summer. Conspicuously fronting the north lawn is the admirably-arranged and finely-furnished Hotel Wentworth. Farther northward, in a leafy recess of great oaks and fragrant evergreens, is the handsomely-built Griffin Institute, which, in all its elaborate features, fitly expresses the unstinted generosity of the highly-esteemed president of the Round Lake Association. Near the hotel is the Round Lake mineral well, the sparkling water of which, as shown by analysis, is like that of the Congress fountain at Saratoga Springs. East of the wood, on a rise of ground commanding a wide prospect of the surrounding country and an extended view of the lake, is the George West Museum of Art and Archæology, a finely-proportioned structure, given the association by its generous treasurer. Garnsey Hall, on Whitfield Avenue, and Kennedy Hall, on Peck Avenue, are also attractive edifices, gifts of the two benevolent women whose names the well-planned buildings bear. Alumni Hall, on Whitfield Avenue, is also a noticeable structure.

PROPRIETARY TITLES OF THE IROQUOIS, FRENCH, DUTCH, AND ENGLISH.

Three centuries ago Round Lake lay within the extensive hunting grounds of the Iroquois or Mohawk Indians. Wild deer browsed in the sunny glades of the great forests environing it, and beavers built their dome-shaped lodges on its bosky banks. Water-fowl found it a haven of rest and refreshment, and in its quiet depths pickerel and other fish abounded.

It was then geographically in New France, near the supposed source of the Grande River (the Hudson), discovered by Giovanni da Verrazzano, in 1524. The French had explored the noble stream as far northward as the site of Waterford, where they bartered for furs with the Mohawk and Mohegan Indians for many years.

Gerard Mercator, the well-known deviser of the projection so serviceable to navigators, was one of the first cartographers to delineate that part of New France, now the territory of New York. On the rare and highly valued map, in the Bibliothèque Nationale, in Paris, made by him in Duisburg, Germany, in 1569, the Grande River is outlined far beyond the height of its navigation at the mouths of the Mohawk. Several ranges of the Adirondack and Green Mountains seen from the high hills at Troy and Lansingburgh are also represented on it to show the natural configuration of the unexplored region in which the great river flowing southward to the sea has its rise.

Forty years later, in the summer of 1609, Samuel de Champlain, the French explorer, penetrated the depths of the vast wilderness, between the St. Lawrence and Mohawk rivers, as far southward as the lake to which he gave his name. At that time the Algonquin Indians of Canada and the Iroquois of New France were at war, and the hunting-grounds of the latter were the field of many conflicts between the warriors of the two hostile tribes. As Champlain was informed by the Algonquins accompanying him, the distance overland to the Grande River from the lake, now known as Lake George, was four leagues. The ambitious Frenchman called the region of country which he had explored Saintonge, the name of his native place in France.

Two months later, Henry Hudson, the English navigator, ascended the Grande River in the "Half Moon." What he learned from the friendly Mohawks respecting the French fur traders is partly disclosed in an inscription on a Dutch map made five years after the exploration of the Grande River, which the Dutch had called the Groote River. "As far as one can understand from what the Maquaas (Mohawks) *say* and *show*, the French come with sloops as high up as their country to trade with them."[1]

After the English had dispossessed the Dutch of New Netherland and had given the name New York to a part of its territory, some of the prominent men of the province began to petition the English Crown to be privileged to buy from the Indians large tracts of land bordering the Hudson and Mohawk Rivers. Among the number of petitioners was Samson Shelton Broughton, Attorney-General of the Province of New York, who, with those associated with him, was licensed April 22d, 1703, to purchase from the Mohawks "a certain

---

[1] *Vide:* The Discoveries of America to the year 1525, by Arthur James Weise, M. A.—G. P. Putnam's Sons, 1884, Chaps. IX., X. and XI.
The History of the City of Albany, New York, by Arthur James Weise, M. A.—E. H. Bender, 1884, Chap. I.

tract of vacant and unappropriated land, in the County of Albany, called or known by the Indian name of Kayarossos," adjoining the north bounds of Schenectady, and extending to the west bounds of Saratoga and to the Hudson River. Overtures were made to some of the Mohawk sachems, who conveyed, October 6th, 1704, as was estimated, from 250,000 to 300,000 acres of land to the persons interested in the purchase. The title to the property was confirmed by a patent granted by Queen Anne, November 2d, 1708.

The so-called Indian name, Kayarossos, or Kayadarossera, as it was written later, said to mean "the country of the lake of the crooked stream," is apparently of French origin, and is evidently a corruption by mispronunciation either of the two French words, *pay arrosé*, a watered country, or of the three, *pay des ruisseaux*, a country of streams.

On the large map of Kayadarossera, made in 1770, and now in the office of the Secretary of State, in the Capitol, in Albany, Round Lake is delineated and designated by its descriptive name. The lake is represented as lying in section two of the ninth allotment.

On some earlier maps the lake is similarly named. The English appellation, Round Lake, displaced the variously written one, Tionoondehowa, Dionoondehowe, Tanendahowa, Shonandohowa, which, it is said, was given the lake by the Indians.

First Camp-Meetings in the United States.

> "The groves were God's first temples. Ere man learned
> To hew the shaft, and lay the architrave,
> And spread the roof above them,—ere he framed
> The lofty vault to gather and roll back
> The sound of anthems,—in the darkling wood,
> Amidst the cool and silence, he knelt down
> And offered to the Mightiest solemn thanks
> And supplications."

No privilege was more heartily enjoyed by the widely-separated settlers cultivating farms in different parts of the United States at the beginning of this century than that of congregating in some accessible wood for a few days in warm weather to listen to the earnest preaching of a number of godly men. One of the earliest of the popular woods' meetings was held in 1799, on the banks of the Red River, in Kentucky. Two brothers, William and John McGee, both preachers, one a Presbyterian and the other a Methodist, came to the settlement there that year and assisted the Rev. James McGready, a Presbyterian minister, in conducting a series of religious services. The meeting-house was not large enough to contain all the people. The zealous men, unwilling to deny themselves the opportunity of preaching to so many hearers, thereupon discoursed from a rudely-constructed platform in an adjacent forest, where the sojourning settlers slept in booths built of the leafy branches of trees or in the wagons in which they had come there.

A year or two later the use of tents instead of booths by some of the people attending the woods' meetings obtained for them the name of camp-meetings.

The first camp-meeting in the State of New York was held at Carmel in 1804. The memorable one at Stillwater, not many miles from Round Lake, in June, 1805, was the first held within the present bounds of the Troy Conference of the Methodist Episcopal Church. It continued four days. The services were conducted by Methodist ministers from Canada, Vermont, Massachusetts, Connecticut, New York, and New Jersey. The presence and preaching of Bishops Asbury and Whatcoat attracted to it great numbers of people, many of whom were converted and became members of the growing church.

In the subsequent period of three and sixty years camp-meetings were annually held at one or more places within the present limits of the Troy Conference. Shortly after the one at Sandlake, in August, 1867, the first steps were taken which led to the purchase of land at Round Lake for the site of a camp-meeting.

Selection of the Round Lake Grounds.

The attractive features and noticeable conveniences of the camp-meeting grounds at Martha's Vineyard induced Joseph Hillman, of Troy, in the summer of 1867, to interest a number of other prominent Methodist laymen in forming an association to purchase an eligible site for a camp-meeting and to provide suitable accommodations for the people attending it. A location along the Troy and Boston Railroad was first searched for, but in consequence of the unwillingness of the officers of the company controlling it to accede to certain proposals made them, the line of the Rensselaer and Saratoga Railroad was then explored for one. Of the places visited none seemed so desirable as a partly-wooded extent of ground between the railroad and Round Lake, seven miles north of Mechanicville.[1]

On September 4th, 1867, the undertaking was further advanced by Joseph Hillman, who that day sent invitations to many Methodist ministers and laymen residing within the limits of the Troy Conference requesting them to attend a meeting to be held on the selected grounds at Round Lake, on Friday, September 20th, and informing them that the morning and afternoon trains from the north and south would stop there then.

The weather was fair on the designated day and a large number of the invited persons was present. Although the aisles of the spacious wood through which they observantly walked were here and there thicket-grown, stone-encumbered, and even marshy in places, the visitors nevertheless admiringly surveyed the symmetrical beauty of the lofty trees, enjoyably inhaled the balsamic fragrance of the evergreens, and appreciatively remarked the natural compactness of the gravelly soil. The advantages of the lake for boating and fishing, the practicability of obtaining an adequate supply of excellent water for drinking and other purposes, and the situation of the grounds at the side of the railroad and at the convergence of several highways further influenced the visitors to decide that the site was in every way suitable for camp-meetings.[2]

---

[1] The pioneers of the enterprise who first viewed the grounds at Round Lake were Joseph Hillman, Gardner Howland, the Rev. C. F. Burdick, and the Rev. Ensign Stover.

[2] The following persons visited the grounds that day: From Troy, Rev. Erastus Wentworth, Rev. John W. Carhart, Rev. Ensign Stover, Rev. M. Hulbard, Joseph Hillman, Perrin W. Converse, Oliver Boutwell, Lyman R. Avery, Ephraim D. Waldron, Leonard Smith, W. L. Van Alstyne, C. Bachelor, N. S. Vedder, Lyman Bennett, William Harris, Gardner Howland, George Bristol, P. S. Pettit, Joseph Crandall, S. J. Peabody, S. L. Wood.

From West Troy, J. D. Lobdell, E. Mors, J. A. Newkirk, C. G. Hill, David Rankin, W. H. Haswell, William Tucker.

From Lansingburgh, Rev. W. R. Brown.

From Waterford, Rev. H. C. Farrar, Levi Dodge, C. E. Howland.

From Cohoes, Rev. H. C. Sexton, Jacob Travis, William Foote.

From Albany, Rev. Jesse T. Peck, D.D., Rev. Dexter E. Clapp, Rev. W. P. Abbott, Rev. Richard Meredith, Rev. I. C. Fenton, Rev. G. C. Wells, Rev. R. H. Robinson, Rev. A. A. Farr, Rev. Charles Devol, M.D., William W. Wollett, William Dalton, D. D. C. Mink, John W. Osborn, S. A. Stratton, B. Nichols, George Downing, Edward Robinson, Lemuel J. Hopkins.

THE ROUND LAKE CAMP-MEETING ASSOCIATION INCORPORATED.

Joseph Hillman, the projector of the enterprise, on May 5th, 1868, obtained the passage of the act by the Legislature of the State of New York, constituting him and his associates the first trustees of the Round Lake Camp-meeting Association of the Methodist Episcopal Church of the Troy Conference.[1] The corporation was permitted to possess real estate not exceeding $150,000 in value and to derive an annual income from its personal property not exceeding $30,000.

The first meeting of the trustees was held at the office of Peck & Hillman, in Troy, on May 4th, 1868. Joseph Hillman was elected President of the Association, Charles W. Pierce, Vice-President, Edgar O. Howland, Secretary, and George Bristol, Treasurer.

On April 1st, 1868, about forty acres of land, lying on the west side of Round Lake, were purchased for the association from Rice Hall and John Moore.

On July 24th, that year, subscriptions to the funds of the association began to be solicited. The work of clearing away the undergrowth in the unfrequented wood was then begun. The removal of the stone fence, running through it from the railroad, and of numerous bowlders roughening the uneven ground was also undertaken.

From a spring on the west side of the railroad water was conveyed by wooden pipes to a pretty fountain in the centre of the space called Fountain Square. Not far eastward of it a covered platform was

---

From Saratoga Springs, Rev. Samuel Meredith, Prof. H. A. Wilson, S. E. Strong, M.D., S S. Strong, M.D., R. Hamilton, M.D.
From Fort Edward, F. D. Hodgeman.
From Ballston Spa, Rev. O. J. Squires, Levi Weed, M.D., Squire Warren.
From Mechanicville, Rev. P. P. Harrower, S. B. Howland, E. O. Howland.
From Stillwater, Rev. S. Brown, Rev. R. Westcott, S. Chase.
From Crescent, Rev. B. M. Hall.
From Clifton Park Village, Rev. A. W. Garvin.
From Greenbush, Rev. T. A. Griffin.
From Center Brunswick, N. B. Betts, Henry Brust.
From Hyndsville, Rev. A. J. Day.
From Williamstown, Mass., S. Southworth.

[1] The first trustees as named in the act were Joseph Hillman, Gardner Howland, George Bristol, Ephraim D. Waldron, Phineas S. Pettit, Hiram A. Wilson, Roscius R. Kennedy, Edgar O. Howland, William Foote, Levi Weed, Robert N. Newton, Charles W. Pierce, Robert Coburn, James H. Earl, William Dalton, F. D. Hodgeman, Joseph E. King, D.D., Hazen W. Bennett, William McEckron, Jesse Wilson, and George L. Clark.

built to be used for a preaching-stand and for sittings for the ministers attending the meetings. In front of it rows of boards, resting on fixed pieces of timber, were arranged to seat the people congregated there during the services. Meanwhile a two-story frame building was erected on the east side of the railroad for a freight and passenger station. These and other improvements preceded the camp-meeting held on the grounds in September.

THE FIRST CAMP-MEETING AT ROUND LAKE.

The first camp-meeting at Round Lake, that of the Troy Conference, was not inaugurated with any special services. On the opening day, Tuesday, September 1st, 1868, the railroad trains brought in the morning and afternoon great numbers of persons who came to remain during the ten days' meeting. Those from the surrounding country arrived in carriages and wagons, bringing with them such movables as were indispensable to dwellers in temporary habitations. While some were busily engaged in pitching and furnishing tents around the space occupied by the platform and rows of seats, others pleasurably strolled through the woods enjoying the freedom of their out-door life. After night-fall a number gathered in front of the preaching-stand, and took part in a prayer-meeting conducted by the Rev. Ensign Stover, of Troy. Two hours later the camp of two hundred and more tents was as silent as the dark woods in which it was embosomed.

The cities of Albany and Troy and the villages northward within the bounds of the Troy Conference all contributed parts of their population to augment the large concourse of people present at the services on the second day. In the morning, at half-past ten o'clock, the Rev. Elisha Watson, Presiding Elder of the Saratoga District of the Troy Conference, having the direction of the exercises, announced from the preachers' stand the regulations of the camp and the order of the daily services. Those of that day were begun by the Rev. C. F. Burdick, Presiding Elder of the Troy District, who announced and read the hymn:

> "Jesus shall reign where'er the sun
> Does his successive journeys run,"

which was sung by the great congregation of more than two thousand persons with that quickened fervor of religious feeling which often animates large bodies of worshipping people. The Rev. J. D. White, of Gansevoort, then offered a prayer, which was followed by the reading of the xix. Psalm by the Rev. Ensign Stover. Then the hymn:

"Jesus, the name high over all,"

read by the Rev. F. A. Soule, of Union Village, was sung. The Rev. Elisha Watson, in behalf of the members of the Round Lake Camp-Meeting Association, then presented the grounds for dedication to the service of God to the Rev. Jesse T. Peck, D.D., of Albany. The subject of his dedicatory discourse was God's revelation of Himself to man as declared by the text, Exodus xx., 24: "In every place where I record my name I will come unto thee, and I will bless thee." The memorable sermon of the eloquent preacher was followed by the dedicatory prayer of the Rev. R. H. Robinson, of Ballston Spa. The singing of the doxology,

Praise God, from whom all blessings flow,

and the giving of the benediction by the Rev. O. J. Squires, of Ballston Spa, closed the impressive services of the morning.

In the afternoon the Rev. John P. Newman, D.D., of New Orleans, preached. He took for his text the interrogation, "Saul, Saul, why persecutest thou me?" In the evening, the Rev. W. P. Abbott, of Albany, discoursed on Isaiah xxi. 11, 12. Prayer meetings were held afterwards in large tents in different parts of the camp.

The presence of more than fifty ministers, some of other denominations, and the attendance of two to three thousand other persons at these first services were gratifying evidences of the success of the association's undertaking.

Public interest in the meetings increased. On Sunday, September 6th, about eight thousand people were on the grounds. On Wednesday evening, September 9th, the sermon of the Rev. Sela W. Brown, of Castleton, on the parable of the wheat and tares, was the last of the thirty discourses delivered during the meeting.[1] The earnest,

---

[1] The following ministers preached: Revs. Jesse T. Peck, D.D., Albany; John P. Newman, D.D., New Orleans; W. P. Abbott, Albany; R. H. Robinson, Ballston Spa; D. P. Hulburd, Jonesville; F. Widmer, Schenectady; Charles Devol, M.D., Albany; —— Ruopp, ——; L. N. Beaudry, Center Brunswick; G. C. Wells, Albany; G. J. Brown, North Adams, Mass.; Ensign Stover, Troy; Carson Parker, Bennington, Vt.; John W. Carhart, Mechanicville; James M. King, Troy; David B. McKenzie, Rock City; J. A. Wood, Wyoming Conference; Erastus Wentworth, D.D., Pittsfield; Simon McChesney, Saratoga Springs; Merritt Hulburd, Troy; J. B. Wood, Clarksville; R. W. Jones, ——; T. S. McMasters, Peru; —— Foote, ——; J. S. Inskip, New York; Ensign Stover, Troy; Benjamin Pomeroy, Waterford; J. C. Wells, Albany; Sela W. Brown, Castleton.

practical, effectual preaching of the Gospel led many hearers to acknowledge and accept Jesus Christ as their Saviour.

One number of the Round Lake *Journal*, edited by the Rev. A. C. Rose, of North Granville, containing telegraphic, general, and local news and advertisements, was issued on Thursday, September 3d.

ROUND LAKE.

A committee from the National Camp-Meeting Association of the Methodist Episcopal Church having visited the grounds during the meeting, and made overtures for the use of them in July, 1869, the Round Lake Camp-Meeting Association accepted the proposals made for the privilege.

The first constitution and by-laws governing the association were adopted September 9th.

On October 20th, that year, the Executive Committee solicited subscriptions by a printed circular, stating that about $17,000 had been expended for land, fences, buildings, tents, water-works and grading, and that it was proposed to make other improvements requiring an outlay of $3,000. Mention was also made that the subscriptions then amounted to nearly $10,000, and that the receipts during the camp-meeting had been $3,365.02, and the expenses $2,020.09.

From the First National to the First Fraternal Camp-Meeting, 1869-1874.

Many of the improvements made by the association in 1869 are represented on a plan of the grounds drawn by H. Drube, a civil engineer, who had surveyed and partly laid them out into building lots and avenues. More than a thousand young trees were planted along the avenues outside the wood and at other points where their shade and growth were thought desirable. Thirteen cottages, mostly two stories high, and eight or ten other buildings were erected.[1]

A bell weighing two hundred pounds was purchased and hung in the tower of the preachers' stand. A bookstore and newsroom, a market and grocery, a post and telegraph office were also eligibly located. For the care, feeding and watering of horses, and for the disposition of vehicles, the arrangements were judicious and ample. Sittings for three thousand people were placed in the auditorium. About four hundred tents, varying in size from the spacious, rainy-weather tent, sufficient for sheltering an audience of more than two thousand persons, to the diminutive sleeping tent, 7 x 7 feet, were provided.

On Tuesday afternoon, July 6th, the introductory sermon of the first meeting of the National Camp-Meeting Association at Round Lake was preached by the Rev. John S. Inskip, of Baltimore, Md., the president of that association. The Rev. M. B. Osborn, of Farmingdale, N. J., delivered the evening discourse.

These and most of the other sermons preached during the meeting were on the subject of holiness, a theme embracing a wide view of the sinfulness of man and of the gracious power of God to elevate him to that higher life opened unto him by Jesus Christ.

The services of Sunday, July 11th, were largely attended, from fifteen to twenty thousand people being present. More than a thousand vehicles and a greater number of horses occupied places assigned them outside the thronged wood. At the morning love feast, at 8 o'clock, testimonies were given by persons living in

---

[1] The nine cottages on Wesley Avenue were erected by Joseph Hillman, Troy; Jacob Travis, Cohoes; R. N. Newton and S. Martin, Albany; Pemble & Wood, Stillwater; Rev. R. H. Robinson, Ballston Spa; Holmes & McEchron, Glens' Falls; James P. Burtis, Mechanicville; F. D. Hodgeman, Fort Edward; E. Lockwood, Mechanicville. The three on Fletcher Avenue, by Steves & Brown, Troy; Cicero Barber, Fort Edward; Sandford Smith, Ballston Spa. The one on Seventh Street, by A. P. Blood, Ballston Spa.

twenty-six states and in the District of Columbia in the United States, and by others living in Canada and in England. At the 10½ o'clock services the Rev. Bishop Matthew Simpson, of Philadelphia, impressively preached to a vast assembly of attentive people. In the afternoon, at 2½ o'clock, five discourses were delivered—one at the preachers' stand, another in the large tent, and a third in Fountain Square, a fourth at the passenger station, and a fifth at the horse-stand.

The presence of more than two hundred and fifty ministers of different denominations at one of the daily services caused not a little comment. Children's meetings were held daily in the large tent. The noted exhorter, "Camp-Meeting John of Maine," frequently took part in the prayer meetings.

On Thursday morning, July 15th, about eighteen hundred persons partook of the elements of the Lord's table in the large tent. On Friday morning following, short addresses, hymns, and prayers terminated this highly successful camp-meeting.[1]

Among the improvements made by the association in July and August, 1869, was the extension northward of Prospect Avenue, and the erection of twelve attractive cottages.[2]

The second camp-meeting of the Troy Conference held on the grounds was one of ten days, beginning on Tuesday, August 31st, conducted by the Rev. C. F. Burdick, Presiding Elder of the Troy District. The first sermon was preached by the Rev. Jesse T. Peck, D.D., of Albany, on Tuesday afternoon, from the text, Hebrews ii., 3: "How shall we escape, if we neglect so great salvation?"

---

[1] The discourses were those of the Revs. John S. Inskip, Baltimore, Md.; W. B. Osborn, Farmingdale, N. J.; W. L. Gray, Philadelphia; W. McDonald, Boston; G. Pratt, Rockland, Me.; Jesse T. Peck, D.D., Albany; Alfred Cookman, Wilmington, Del.; C. Munger, Bath, Me.; J. W. Horne, New York City; William Butler, Boston, Sec. American and Foreign Christian Union; W. Reddy, Utica; Rev. Bishop M. Simpson, Philadelphia; Andrew Longacre, New York City; G. Hughes, Hightstown, N. J.; ——— Chapman, Philadelphia; G. C. Wells, Albany; S. Coleman, Williamsport, Pa.; Lewis R. Dunn, Jersey City; W. H. Boole, Williamsburgh, N. Y.; John Cookman, New York City; ——— Lawrence, N. J.

[2] One on Ninth Street, erected by the Rev. E. Stover, Troy; two on Fletcher Avenue, by Dr. S. S. Strong and Prof. H. A. Wilson, Saratoga Springs, and E. A. Hartshorn, Troy; one on Tenth Street, by Charles Smith, M.D., Albany; one on Albany Street, by Rev. F. A. Soule, Sandy Hill; seven on Wesley avenue, by H. J. Porter, M.D., Bennington, Vt.; L. M. Smith, Half Moon; S. F. Harris, Bennington, Vt.; Miss Margaret C. Clement, Half Moon; Henry Howarth, Cohoes; James Heimstreet, Cohoes; Walter Witbeck, Cohoes.

The number of people occupying tents was large. The daily services were well-attended and the preaching was forcible and effective.[1] The meetings to promote entire consecration to God were in charge of Mrs. Sarah Lankford, of Brooklyn.

The general attractiveness of the grounds in the month of June, 1870, was much admired by the people attending the third Troy Conference camp-meeting at Round Lake. The fresh and perfect foliage of the trees, the bright verdure of the lawns, and the inviting appearance of the embowered cottages elicited the comment of all. The latest improvements included the Bishop's cottage, erected on the east side of Wesley Avenue.[2] Tuesday, June 21st, had been announced for the beginning of the camp-meeting, conducted by the Rev. Samuel Meredith, Presiding Elder of the Albany District, but the accidental detention on the railroad cars of the minister designated to preach that evening caused the first services to be postponed to Wednesday morning. The introductory sermon was by the Rev. Ensign Stover, of West Troy.

The holding of the meeting in June was evidently unwise, for at that time farmers were most actively engaged in agriculture, and therefore debarred from attending the services. The absence of the country people was noticeable in the comparatively small number of persons daily congregated on the grounds. On Sunday, June 26th, about two thousand people were present at the morning and afternoon services. On the following Tuesday morning the Rev. Bishop E. S. Janes, of New York City, preached an excellent sermon. The camp-meeting closed on Friday morning, July 1st, with a love feast.[3]

[1] Sermons were preached by the Revs. Jesse T. Peck, Albany; R. H. Robinson, Ballston Spa; D. W. Gates, Cambridge; A. Ford, Stillwater; E. Stover, Troy; Homer Eaton, West Troy; J. R. Henderson, Lima, Ohio; E. A. Blanchard, Clifton Park Village; R. Meredith, North Adams, Mass.; G. S. Chadbourne, Gloversville; S. W. Brown, Waterford; ———— Steves; H. C. Sexton, Saratoga Springs; J. M. Webster, Greenfield; Erastus Wentworth, Pittsfield; W. G. Waters, Albany; Louis N. Beaudry, Albany; S. Meredith, Albany, Presiding Elder of Albany District; G. C. Wells, Albany; Merritt Hulburd, Troy.

[2] Three other cottages had been erected on Wesley Avenue severally belonging to the Rev. William Griffin, D.D., of West Troy; Gardner Howland, of Troy; and the Rev. B. D. Ames, of Mechanicville.

[3] The sermons preached during the meeting were by the Revs. Ensign Stover, West Troy; R. H. Robinson, Ballston Spa; J. R. Wager, Green Island; M. D. Jessup, West Amsterdam; F. A. Soule, Sandy Hill; J. Belknap, Pittstown; Homer Eaton, West Troy; J. W. Tucker, Troy; Jesse T. Peck, D.D., Syracuse; Merritt

The fourth Troy Conference camp-meeting at Round Lake, conducted by the Rev. Elisha Watson, Presiding Elder of the Saratoga District, began on Monday, September 5th, 1870. About four hundred persons attended the evening services, at which the Rev. Abel Ford, of Stillwater, preached the initial sermon of the meeting. The services of the week were variably attended, several hundred to two thousand persons being present from day to day. The meeting inmforally closed on Saturday, September 10th, the weather being stormy.[1]

The sixth camp-meeting held at Round Lake was that of the National Camp-Meeting Association in 1871, conducted by its president, the Rev. John S. Inskip, of Baltimore. About three hundred and fifty tents were pitched around the audience center, and they and the thirty and more cottages accommodated the sojourners from ten different states, numbering from one to two thousand persons and representing many of the different Christian denominations in the United States. The object of the meeting was the promotion of holiness. At one of the daily services three ministers, one a Methodist, one a Congregationalist and the third a Baptist, all doctors of divinity, officiated.

On Tuesday afternoon, July 4th, the Rev. John S. Inskip preached the first sermon. In the evening, on account of the rain, there was no sermon. Services of prayer, praise, and exhortation were held in the large tent.

At the eight o'clock love feast on Sunday morning, three hundred and seventy-seven persons spoke of their Christian experience within an hour and forty-five minutes. About ten thousand people attended the morning and afternoon services that day. Not less than two

Hulburd, Albany; L. Marshall, Cohoes; D. P. Hulburd, Jonesville; Joseph E. King, D.D., Fort Edward; B. B. Loomis, Mechanicville; B. M. Hall, Rutland, Vt.; R. Meredith, Brooklyn; J. E. Irvine, Dingman's Ferry, N. J.; Bishop E. S. Janes, New York City; D. B. McKenzie, Bethlehem; D. Hawley, D.D., Glens' Falls; S. McChesney, Albany; H. W. Slocum, Brunswick; Louis N. Beaudry, Albany; G. W. Brown, Troy; G. H. Townsend, Pittsford, Vt.

[1] The following ministers preached during the meeting: Revs. Abel Ford, Stillwater; J. C. Fenton, Watervliet; R. Wheatley, Hudson; J. M. Webster, Rock City; Erastus Wentworth, D.D., Pittsfield, Mass.; C. K. True, Springfield, Mass.; D. B. McKenzie, Bethlehem; Samuel Meredith, Presiding Elder of the Albany District; Bishop Jesse T. Peck, Syracuse; D. T. Elliott, Sandlake; Benjamin Pomeroy, Albany; Simon McChesney, Albany; S. W. Brown, Waterford.

thousand persons were present at the Monday morning prayer-meeting, at five o'clock.

The closing sacramental services on Thursday evening, July 13th, were attended by about three thousand persons. The singing of the hymn

"All hail the power of Jesus' name,"

terminated this signally blessed camp meeting.[1]

The use of the grounds for residence during the months of summer by those owning or renting the cottages was proposed in 1872. About forty had been erected.[2] In order to ascertain the acceptableness of the privilege, the following announcement was made by the association in the spring of that year: " Believing that the use of the grounds for summer homes for Christian families cannot in any way interfere with, but rather promote the spirituality of the camp-meetings, the trustees have declared a ' Season,' commencing July 1st, and continuing until October 1st, during which time the morning and evening trains each way will stop for the accommodation of those who desire to remain upon the grounds, provided a sufficient number remains."

[1] The sermons were by the Revs. John S. Inskip, Baltimore, Md.; William McDonald, Brooklyn; W. L. Gray, Philadelphia; A. McLean, New York; W. S. Harlow, Duxbury, Mass.; G. C. Wells, Milwaukee; W. H. Boole, New York; L. R. Dunn, Elizabeth, N. J.; J. W. Horne, Babylon N. Y.; Andrew Longacre, New York; W. H. Hughes, ———; J. E. Searles, New York; Alfred Cookman, Newark; C. Munger, Alford, Mass.; Seymour Coleman, ———; Edgar M. Levy, D.D., Philadelphia; W. Reddy, D.D., Skeneateles; James Porter, Boston, Mass.; ——— Lee, New York; C. D. Foss, New York.

[2] The cottages were owned by the following persons: The Bishop's by the association; Rev. William Griffin, D.D., West Troy; Joseph Hillman, Troy; Gardner Howland, Troy; J. P. Burtis, Minnesota; J. A. S. Lord, Albany; D. C Holman, Glens' Falls; F. D. Hodgeman, Fort Edward; Rev. Joseph E. King, D.D., Fort Edward; George West, Ballston Spa; R. N. Newton and S. Martin, Albany; Rev. B. O. Ames, Mechanicville; Jacob Travis, Cohoes; John Burhans, Galway; L. M. Smith, Clifton Park; Miss M. C. Clement, Clifton Park; H. Haworth, Cohoes; J. Heimstreet, Cohoes; Henry Brust, Brunswick; W. Witbeck, Cohoes; L. Wood, Stillwater; L. N. Beaudry, Shelbourne Falls, Vt., and H. A. Wolf, Greenbush; ——— Stockwell and ——— Huling, Bennington; Mrs. Harriet Bradley, Schenectady; S. F. Harris, Bennington; Dr. H. J. Petter, Bennington; Dr. S. S. Strong and Prof. H. A. Wilson, Saratoga Springs; E. A. Hartshorn and Moses Hovey, Troy; A. C. Fellows, Troy; Cicero Barber, Fort Edward; Rev. J. W. Belknap, Petersburgh; Sanford Smith, Fort Edward; A. P. Blood, Ballston Spa; Jesse Wilson, Hampton; Haight and Mosher, Stillwater; Dr. C. H. Smith, Albany; Eleazer A. Peck, Troy; Mrs. E. Stover, Saratoga Springs; Rev. A. Osborn, Hagaman's Mills Mrs. Almira Waterman, Brooklyn.

Few of the previous camp-meetings held at Round Lake were as remarkable in interesting incidents as the first New York State meeting in July, 1872. The discourses were thoughtful, earnest, and impressive, and the exhortations direct and urgent. Deep feeling and fervent longings for spiritual blessings notably characterized the prayer meetings. Amanda Smith, an intelligent negro woman, once a slave, being present for the first time at Round Lake attending the varied services of this meeting, enlisted the attention of many impenitent persons by her sympathetic singing and cogent reasoning concerning the importance of living a Christian life.

The opening sermon was preached on Tuesday evening, July 16th, by the Rev. B. I. Ives, of Auburn, New York, who had charge of the meeting. On the following Sunday, about one thousand vehicles and more than ten thousand people entered the grounds. Including those at the preachers' stand, there were no less than thirty-three religious meetings held that day at different places in the enjoyable shade of the spacious wood. On Thursday night, at ten o'clock, most of the three thousand persons attending the evening services partook of the Lord's Supper. After the usual march around the "circle," the seventh camp-meeting held at Round Lake was closed at midnight with a benediction[1].

The new and attractive passenger station at Round Lake, built in the spring of 1873, by the Delaware and Hudson Canal Company, lessee of the Rensselaer and Saratoga Railroad, was one of the most conspicuous of the improvements made that year. It was constructed of corrugated, galvanized iron. The middle part, containing the ticket-office, waiting and baggage rooms, is twenty-four feet wide and forty long, and the open wings, north and south, are twenty by seventy feet. The uncomfortable plank seats in the audience-space

---

[1] The following ministers preached during the meeting: Revs. B. I. Ives, Auburn; L. N. Beaudry, Shelburne Falls, Vt.; Charles F. Noble, Troy; G. S. White, Utica; S. D. Brown, New York; R. A. Caruthers, Presiding Elder of the Fredonia District, Erie Conference; W. N. Cobb, Presiding Elder of Otsego District; Joseph E. King, D.D., Fort Edward; S. W. Brown, West Troy; S. Meredith, Troy; Seymour Coleman, ———; B. Pomeroy, Troy; ——— Butler, Secretary of Board for the Conversion of Roman Catholics; A. J. Kynett, D.D., Philadelphia; D. D. Lindsley, Presiding Elder of the Oswego District of the Wyoming Conference; J. B. Wakeley, of Newburgh District; ——— Teed, of Rock River Conference; H. Skeel, of Saquoit; J. B. Foote, Presiding Elder of Syracuse District; J. C. Fenton, Bath; C. S. Clement, North Bennington, Vt.

were removed, and backed benches placed in front of the preachers' stand. The purchase of the Corps farm and of land lying on the north and east sides of the grounds increased their area to 120 acres, with a frontage of nearly a half mile on the lake. An avenue extending from the central part of the grounds to the lake was laid out and a boat-landing constructed at the termination of the new road.

The second New York State camp-meeting, conducted by the Rev. B. I. Ives, of Auburn, was informally opened with a prayer meeting on Tuesday evening, July 8th, 1873. On Wednesday morning the Rev. B. I. Ives preached the first sermon. The closing of the gates on the following Sunday limited the attendance at the services to those persons sojourning on the grounds. The large tent purchased by the association, in which to hold services in rainy weather, was dedicated on Saturday afternoon, July 12th. From three to four thousand people were present at the services on the following Tuesday. Twenty-two ministers preached during the meeting, among whom was Bishop Peck[1]. Sacramental services were held at nine o'clock on Thursday evening, July 17th, and after "the walk about Jerusalem," this eighth camp-meeting held at Round Lake was closed with a benediction.

In the summer of 1873, the new highway, named Waugh Avenue, on the west side of the lake, was completed, and the old road running along the line of Janes Avenue closed. The former was accepted by the Commissioners of Highways of the town of Malta on Saturday, August 30th. The superintendent's house, on the southeast corner of Lake and Hedding Avenues, was among the number of new buildings erected in the summer.

The fifth camp-meeting of the Troy Conference held on the grounds began on Wednesday morning, September 3d, 1873, the Rev. Sanford Washburn, of Jonesville, conducting it. The morning's sermon was preached by the Rev. S. M. Williams, of Schuylerville. Twenty-two other discourses were delivered during the meeting by

---

[1] The ministers who preached were the Revs. B. I. Ives, Auburn; J. M. Webster, Presiding Elder of the Cambridge District; Alexander Campbell, of Troy Conference; Bishop Jesse T. Peck; J. F. Yates, Chenango; H. Wheeler, Presiding Elder of Otsego District; Bostwick Hawley, D.D., Bennington, Vt.; Merritt Hulburd, Springfield, Mass.; L. N. Beaudry, Shelburne, Vt.; G. W. Knapp, Claverack; Joseph E. King, D.D., Fort Edward; William Adams, of Central New York Conference; A. A. Farr, Albany; S. W. Brown, West Troy; J. B. Hammond, Chateaugay; David H. Muller, Rochester; S. W. Clemens, Greenbush; L. R. Thayer, Springfield, Mass.; S. Meredith, Troy; D. Austin, Frey's Bush; J. M. Edgerton, Sandy Hill; —— Shepard, ——.

different ministers.[1] On Sunday, September 7th, the gates were closed, and about two thousand persons were denied admittance to to the grounds.

ALUMNI HALL.

The judiciousness of debarring the public from the grounds on Sunday had frequently been discussed. The gates at first were never

[1] Revs. I. C. Fenton, Greenbush; Peter M. Hitchcock, Cooksborough; W. J. Sands, Guilderland; M. D. Jump, Valatie; B. F. Livingston, Castleton; O. Gregg, Presiding Elder of the Burlington District; George C. Morehouse, Mechanicville; W. J. Tilley, Dalton; S. W. Edgerton, Dannemora; H. D. Kimball, Williamstown, Mass.; A. F. Bailey, Troy; Robert Patterson, Crescent; A. D. Head, ——— ———; E. Marsh, Kinderhook; M. A. Senter, South Adams, Mass.; Thomas Kelley, Mooers; M. B. Mead, Lansingburgh; H. W. Slocum, Brunswick; S. W. Clemens, Greenbush; R. J. Adams, Johnsonville; William Bedell, Tomhannock; Seymour Coleman.

closed. No little ill-feeling was therefore engendered by the enforcement of the regulation denying entrance to the grounds on Sunday. After this meeting certain modifications changed the restrictions and the gates were opened. The meeting closed on Friday evening, July 12th.

From the First Fraternal Camp-Meeting to the First Sunday School Assembly, 1874–1877.

The most notable of all the meetings held at Round Lake was the Fraternal meeting in 1874. The leaven of its wonderful influence permeated the great body of the Methodist Church in the United States and widely quickened the growth of good will among the ministers and laity of its different branches. It noticeably brought into closer relations the interests of the two divisions of the church, North and South, that had so long been separated by political differences respecting slavery and the bitter feeling caused by the Civil War.

Fortunately, in the spring of 1874, the project of holding a fraternal camp-meeting at Round Lake, to which the bishops, ministers, and laymen of the different branches of the church should be invited, occurred to the liberal-minded and indefatigable president of the association, Joseph Hillman. He disclosed his conception of the benefits of the meeting to the Rev. Bishop Simpson in Philadelphia, who, besides approving the project, advised him to consult with the Rev. Bishop Janes, residing in New York City, who had been elected to his bishoprick by the votes of the representatives from the southern states. Bishop Janes at once expressed his willingness to co-operate with the officers of the association in securing the desired attendance of those to be invited to the proposed meeting. He thereupon wrote the invitation, signed by the Presiding Elders of the Troy Conference, setting forth the high purpose of the meeting, and the letter of acceptance to which so many of the bishops willingly subscribed their names, and also the paper bearing the signatures of the large number of representative men of the church who signified their intention of being present. Taking with him the invitation of the Presiding Elders of the Troy Conference, the two other papers, and a letter of introduction written by the Rev. Bishop Janes, the earnest president of the Round Lake Camp-Meeting Association visited Louisville, Ky., where, in May, 1874, the General Conference of the Methodist Church South was in session. The incidents of the different interviews which he held with the officers of the conference and other representatives of the church south and their interrogations, made his mission one of extreme delicacy and prudent action. The success of his efforts, besides being agreeably disclosed in the published acceptances of the invitations given them, was later more gratifyingly expressed in the presence of the large body of bishops, eminent ministers, and prominent laymen of the Methodist Church South at the Fraternal meeting, the purpose of which, as Bishop Janes wrote, was "not to talk about fraternity, but to enjoy it; not to plan for it, but to practice it."

The accommodations for the comfort and entertainment of the people attending the meeting, which began on July 8th, and continued fourteen days, were in every way sufficient and satisfactory. Eight or ten churches had tabernacles in which to lodge many of their members. The public boarding tents were enlarged to seat at the tables more than five hundred persons at one time. Wreaths of evergreen were festooned around the preachers' stand, and along the back part of it a long piece of canvas displayed the inscription, "Behold how good and how pleasant it is for brethren to dwell together in unity." Across some of the avenues scriptural texts were suspended. The most remarked of these was the one, "I will say to the North, Give up; and to the South, Keep not back."

Representatives of ten branches of the Methodist Church in North America were present at this memorable meeting. Bishops Janes, Simpson, Foster, Haven, and Peck of the Methodist Episcopal Church; Bishops Kavanaugh and Doggett, of the Methodist Episcopal Church South; Bishop Campbell, of the African Methodist Episcopal Church; and Bishops Jones and Clinton, of the African Methodist Episcopal Zion Church, all took prominent parts in the varied and impressive services. During the fourteen days of the meeting (some of them rainy) more than fifty sermons were preached by ministers from different parts of the United States and Canada.[1]

[1] The sermons were by Bishop E. S. Janes, D.D., LL.D., New York City; Thomas B. Sargent, Baltimore, Md.; Anson Green, D.D., Toronto, Canada; Bishop J. P. Campbell, Philadelphia, Pa.; Joseph Cummings, D.D., LL.D., Middletown, Conn.; T. M. Eddy, D.D., New York City; ———— Plummer, D.D., ————, Tenn.; Joseph Dare, Melbourne, Australia; John S. Inskip, ————; Bishop M. Simpson, D.D., Philadelphia, Pa.; S. V. Leech, Baltimore, Md.; S. Call, ————, N. Y.; William Reddy, D.D., Syracuse, ————; Isaac McCann, ————, ————; F. Bottome, D.D., New York City; L. H. King, D.D., New York City; W. C. Henderson, Stratford, Canada; T. H. Pearne, D.D., Cincinnati, Ohio; A. L. Cooper, D.D., St. Albans, Vt.; F. Widmer, Carthage, N. Y.; J. M. Walden,

On Wednesday evening, July 8th, the Rev. Bishop Janes, D.D., LL.D., who had charge of the meeting, preached the first sermon, the subject being, "The adaptedness of Christianity to man's spiritual necessities," and the text, 1. Cor., i., 30.

The hymns, "Christian Greeting," by Mrs. Joseph Hillman, "The Day of Days," by the Rev. F. Bottome, D.D.; "Devotion," by Eleazer A. Peck, and "Christian Unity," by the Rev. A. C. Rose, written for the occasion, were sung at the Thursday morning services.

On the following Sunday it rained. Seventeen sermons were preached that day at different places on the grounds.

By invitation, Ulysses S. Grant, President of the United States of America, visited Round Lake on Wednesday, July 15th. He arrived on the morning train from Saratoga Springs, between nine and ten o'clock, and was taken to the Bishop's cottage. Shortly afterward he was escorted to the preachers' stand, where he was introduced to the people congregated there by the Rev. Bishop Janes, and was received with prolonged hand-clapping. Seated on the stand, the President heard the sermon preached by the Rev. George Douglass, D.D., of Montreal, Canada, on the Power and Assurance of the Gospel. After dining at one of the boarding tents and holding a short reception in front of the preachers' stand, the President departed on a special train for Saratoga Springs.

The services were well attended. Often the number of ministers present exceeded a hundred and of the laity five thousand.

On Wednesday morning, July 22d, this first Fraternal camp-meeting at Round Lake terminated with a love feast.

The good-will which this meeting established between the two great bodies of the Methodist Church North and South led to the

D.D., Cincinnati, Ohio; C. C. McCabe, D.D., Chicago, Ill.; J. B. Foote, Syracuse, N. Y.; J. T. Walker, D.D., ———; William McDonald, ———; J. L. Gilder, New York City; Sela W. Brown, Galesburgh, Ill.; Lewis R. Dunn, Paterson, N. J.; J. Gardner, D.D., Hamilton, Canada; John B. McFerrin, D.D., Nashville, Tenn.; John J. Murray, D.D., Pittsburgh, Pa.; D. D. Lore, D.D., Syracuse, N. Y.; Bishop H. H. Kavanaugh, D.D., Louisville, Ky.; John Potts, D.D., Toronto, Canada; George Douglass, D.D., Montreal, Canada; L. W. Bates, D.D., Baltimore, Md.; John Poisal, D.D., Baltimore, Md.; A. J. Kynett, D.D., Philadelphia, Pa.; L. D. White, Potsdam, N. Y.; E. O. Haven, D.D., LL.D., Syracuse, N. Y.; Charles F. Deems, D.D., New York City; Bishop Jesse T. Peck, D.D., San Francisco, Cal.; William Hunter, D.D., Pittsburgh, Pa.; Bishop R. S. Foster, D.D., LL.D., Cincinnati, Ohio; Leroy M. Lee, D.D., Richmond, Va.; Bishop D. S. Doggett, D.D., Richmond, Va.; Cyrus D. Foss, D.D., New York City; Bishop Gilbert Haven, D.D., Atlanta, Ga.; B. I. Ives, Auburn, N. Y.; Alexander Clark, D.D., Pittsburgh, Pa.; Bishop S. T. Jones, Washington, D. C.

appointment of a commission by their respective conferences to harmonize their interests. The commissioners met at Cape May, N. J., and amicably determined the adjustment of the long-existing differences. Bishop Pierce in a letter to the General Conference of the Methodist Episcopal Church South, wrote with marked emphasis that the Fraternal meeting at Round Lake was the chief factor in settling them.

At the close of the first Fraternal camp-meeting in July, 1874, the Presiding Elders of the Troy Conference and the Trustees of the Round Lake Camp-Meeting Association were requested by the bishops and many of the ministers and laymen attending the services to appoint a similar meeting to be held in July, 1875. The desire of the signers of the request was at once complied with and a general invitation extended to "the great family of Methodists" in North America to a second fraternal gathering on the grounds at the designated time.

One of the incidents of the summer was the launching of a small steamboat, to which the name "Ordelia," the name of the wife of the president of the association, Mrs. Joseph Hillman, was given. The vessel was forty-five feet long and carried forty passengers. A yacht and about fifteen row-boats were also owned by the association. A new boat-house was erected on the north side of the landing at the foot of Covel Avenue.

The area of the grounds was greatly enlarged by the purchase of sixty-five acres of land on the west side of the railroad, and subsequently of fifteen acres on the north side of the property, east of the railroad, the entire area of the grounds being about two hundred acres. Avenues and building lots were laid out on a part of the later purchased property, and a new map of the grounds was printed in the Round Lake *Journal* issued in June, 1875.

The presence of nine bishops and the frequent attendance of thousands of people made the second Fraternal camp-meeting nearly equal to the first one in distinction. The first of the series of excellent sermons was preached on Thursday evening, July 1st, 1875, by the Rev. Joseph E. King, D.D., of Fort Edward. The meeting was conducted by the Rev. Bishop E. S. Janes, D.D., of New York City. During its continuance about thirty-five discourses were delivered by ministers representing different branches of the Methodist Church in the United States and Canada.

[1] The following ministers preached: Revs. Joseph E. King, Fort Edward; S. V. Leech, Baltimore, Md.; L. N. Beaudry, Green Island; Hiram Dunn, Schroon

Assured by eminent geologists that mineral water similar to that of the springs at Saratoga could be obtained by boring through the strata of the Hudson River shale, the Round Lake Camp-Meeting Association employed Conde & Denton to drill a well near the southwest corner of Burlington and George avenues. On Saturday noon, July 10th, a number of people assembled there to witness the beginning of the undertaking. The following poetical composition was written and read by the Rev. Joseph E. King, D.D., of Fort Edward, entitled:

SMITING THE ROCK.

'Tis a fair scene to-day that greets our sight,
Thanks be to God, who gives the precious light.
That glorious grove beneath whose grateful shade
The fair white tents of Israel are made,
Where hungry multitudes are daily fed
With manna from the bending heavens shed,
Whose grand, green arches ring with sacred song,
Till all the conscious leaves the strains prolong.
Yon peaceful lake, that mirrors back the sky,
Like Christian hearts, when Jesus passeth by,—
Where on the earth can lovelier spot be found?
With grateful joy we call it holy ground.
Be sure of this, the skeptic jeers despite,
The smiling earth is not a hypocrite.
If on the surface Nature is so fair,
Beneath that surface must be treasures rare.
Stir with a vigorous hoe her generous soil,
And laughing harvests will reward your toil.
Deep in her entrails he doth find that bores
For light and fuel, more than kingly stores.
At Saratoga, by many a gushing spout,
In floods she pours her healing waters out.
We, too, for healing waters are in quest,
And come to Mother Nature's bounteous breast
To pierce, mayhap, some deep, all-healing rill,
And in this hope and faith, we start "*the drill*,"
Be this to us instead of Moses' rod,
And when the waters flow the praise shall be to God.

Lake; C. F. Burdick, Presiding Elder of Albany District; Bishop W. L. Harris, D.D., Chicago, Ill.; ——— Register, Baltimore, Md.; Bishop E. G. Andrews, D.D., Des Moines, Ia.; A. S. Hunt, D.D., Brooklyn, N. Y.; W. H. Hunter, D.D., ; ——— Spear, D.D., , Ky.; Bishop Miles, ; Bishop J. P. Campbell, African M. E. Church, Philadelphia, Pa.; J. F. Clymer, Glens' Falls; Bishop Halsey (African), , Ga.; P. A. Moelling, D.D., Troy, N. Y.; J. T. Murray, D.D., Newark, N. J.; ——— Wiley, D.D.,

After some happy remarks respecting the enterprise of the association had been made by the Rev. John P. Newman, D.D., of Washington, D. C., the drilling machinery was set in operation.

Amanda Smith, of Philadelphia, was on the grounds during the meeting, and heartily engaged in the religious exercises in the prayer-meeting tents. Mrs. Sarah Lankford, of Brooklyn, was also a zealous co-worker.

About two thousand persons, bishops, ministers and laymen, marched in procession, singing farewell hymns at the close of the meeting on Wednesday morning, July 14th.

COTTAGE OF REV. WILLIAM GRIFFIN, D.D.

The display of flags at the preachers' stand and on most of the cottages at the opening of the third Fraternal camp-meeting on Fri-

; T. H. Pearne, D.D., Cincinnati, Ohio; Bishop R. S. Foster, D.D., Cincinnati, Ohio; John P. Newman, D.D., Washington, D. C.; J. O. Clarke, D.D., Savannah, Ga.; Cyrus D. Foss, D.D., New York City; Bishop H. H. Kavanaugh, D.D., Louisville, Ky.; A. R. Sanford, D.D., Prattsville, N. Y.; Bishop I. W. Wiley, D.D., Boston, Mass.. J. B. McFerrin, D.D., Nashville, Tenn.; J. Hunt, , Canada; John Shaw, D.D., , Canada; Bishop S. T. Jones, African M. E. Church, Philadelphia; Bishop Thomas Bowman, D.D., St. Louis, Mo.; E. J. Drinkhouse, D.D., Baltimore; F. Bottome, D.D., New York City; A. J. Kynett, D.D., Philadelphia.

day morning, June 23d, 1876, signalized the centennial year of the signing of the Declaration of Independence. The services of this meeting were under the direction of the Rev. Bishop E. S. Janes. The Rev. D. T. Elliott, of Charlton, N. Y., delivered the first of the twenty-eight discourses heard by the large congregations present at the services. Bishops Janes, Peck, Simpson, Foster, and Wayman, and other eminent ministers of the church from different parts of the country, officiated in them.[1] Many of the persons attending the meeting enjoyed the daily excursions around the lake in the "Ordelia" and the barge "Centennial," towed by her. The services closed on Monday, July 4th, with an experience meeting.

In the summer, a canvas canopy to shelter the congregated people in rainy weather was purchased by the association and extended over framework above the seats in the auditorium-space. A bell of six hundred pounds weight was placed in the tower on the preachers' stand.

The sixth Conference camp-meeting began on Tuesday evening, September 5th, 1876, with a service of praise and prayer, and remarks by some of the ministers present. On Wednesday morning, the Rev. Homer Eaton, Presiding Elder of the Albany District, who had charge of the meeting, preached the initial sermon. The daily afternoon services were assigned to Mrs. Maggie Van Cott, of New York City, the distinguished evangelist, whose earnest and impressive preaching attracted to the grounds not infrequently from four to five thousand people. On Sunday, September 10th, four hundred and eighty-seven teams entered the gates, which had been closed on Sundays for several years. Besides the discourses of Mrs. Van Cott,

---

[1] Sermons were preached by Revs. D. T. Elliott, Charlton, N. Y.; E. C. Curtiss, D.D., Syracuse, N. Y.; J. H. Coleman, Galway, N. Y.; H. D. Kimball, Troy, N. Y.; William Bedell, Troy, N. Y.; G. C. Morehouse, Poultney, Vt.; Bishop E. S. Janes, D.D., New York City; J. B. McFerrin, D.D., Nashville, Tenn.; G. C. Bancroft, Troy, N. Y.; S. V. Leech, D.D., Baltimore, Md.; S. Coleman, Williamsport, Pa.; Bishop Jesse T. Peck, D.D., San Francisco, Cal.; A. K. Sanford, D.D., Prattsville, N. Y.; D. B. McKenzie, Hampton; Bishop A. W. Wayman, D.D., African Methodist Episcopal Church, Baltimore, Md.; T. A. Griffin, Presiding Elder of the Plattsburgh District; John Duncan, a blind clergyman, Ga.; Bishop M. Simpson, D.D., Philadelphia, Pa.; John Poisal, D.D., Baltimore, Md.; A. Schriver, Coeyman's Hollow, N. Y.; Bishop R. S. Foster, D D., Cincinnati, Ohio; ——— Ware, Va.; Duncan, D.D., President of Randolph Macon College, Wynona, Va.; J. M. Thoburn, D.D , Bengal Presidency, India; ——— Clarke Savannah, Ga.; L. H. King, Newburgh, N. Y.; ——— Wiley, D.D., Madison, N. J.

fifteen sermons were delivered by ministers of the Troy Conference and by several Methodist clergymen from distant places.[1]

On Monday morning, September 11th, at ten o'clock, a spring of mineral water was penetrated by the drill at a depth of more than thirteen hundred feet from the surface of the ground. Late in the afternoon several gallons of turbid water were drawn from the well in the presence of a crowd of interested spectators, when the water was found to be similar in taste to that of the Congress Spring at Saratoga Springs. Mrs. Van Cott began singing the long meter doxology, in which she was joined by the persons standing near her. Congratulatory remarks were made by the Rev. L. H. King, D.D., of Newburgh, N. Y.; the Rev. Homer Eaton, Albany; Joseph Hillman, President of the Round Lake Camp-Meeting Association, and by John D. Rogers, the superintendent of the grounds.[2] Subsequently, when the well was drilled to the depth of fourteen hundred and three feet and was tubed, the water was submitted to Prof. Charles F. Chandler, of Columbia College, whose analysis indicated that its composition differed little from the water of the Congress Spring at Saratoga Springs.

On Thursday evening, September 16th, this thirteenth camp-meeting held at Round Lake ended with a sacramental service. Farewells were taken, with hand-shaking, and the singing of

> "Amen, amen, my soul replies,
> I'm bound to meet you in the skies,
> And claim my mansion there;
> Now here's my heart and here's my hand
> To meet you in that heavenly land,
> Where we shall part no more."

[1] They were the Revs. Homer Eaton, Albany; W. J. Heath, Burlington, Vt.; S. Meredith, Troy; L. N. Beaudry, Montreal, Canada; Rev. W. Butler, D.D., Mexico; A. F. Bailey, Schuylerville, N. Y.; P. Krohn, Albany; D. W. Foster, ——; B. I. Ives, Auburn, N. Y.; John P. Newman, D.D., Washington, D. C.; M. D. Jump, Williamstown, Mass.; D. T. Elliott, Charlton, N. Y.; L. H. King, D.D., Newburgh; W. H. Meeker, Cohoes; Erastus Wentworth, D.D., Sandy Hill; Samuel McLaughlin, Albany.

[2] The sample of mineral water submitted to me for examination contains, in one U. S. gallon of 231 cubic inches:

Chloride of Sodium................................	394.2943 grains.
" Potassium..................	9.4363 "
Bromide of Sodium..........................	1.4716 "
Iodide of Sodium..................................	1.3152 "
Fluoride of Sodium	trace.

The extension of Burlington Avenue to the new gateway on the north side of the grounds, the erection of a number of cottages,[1] and the connection of the two public dining halls by the removal of the intermediate walls were some of the noticeable improvements made prior to the Union Evangelistic camp-meeting held at Round Lake in July, 1877.

The services of the Union Evangelistic camp-meeting were conducted by the Rev. S. H. Platt, a distinguished Methodist minister from Brooklyn, N. Y. On Tuesday morning, July 10th, a love feast inaugurated the exercises of the day. In the afternoon the Rev. Daniel Steel, D.D., of Lynn, Mass., preached the first sermon. The fifteen and more discourses delivered by the Revs. T. DeWitt Talmage, John P. Newman, D.D., O. H. Tiffany, D.D., A. B. Earle, E. P. Hammond, and other eminent divines and noted evangelists of different Christian denominations contributed to make the meeting one of special interest and importance.[2] The number of persons present at the services on Sunday morning and afternoon, July 15th,

Bicarbonate of Lithia	2.7494	grains.
" Soda	48.9871	"
" Magnesia	9.7846	"
" Lime	13.4457	"
" Strontia	1.2038	"
" Baryta	0.5520	"
" Iron	0.6344	"
" Manganese	0.0768	"
Sulphate of Potassa	1.0275	"
Phosphate of Soda	0.0228	"
Biborate of Soda	trace.	
Alumina	0.0316	"
Silica	1.2247	"
Organic Matter	trace.	
	486.2608	
Density	1.0059.	

C. F. CHANDLER,
Chemist and Assayer.

NEW YORK, August 2d, 1878.

[1] The new cottages were those of A. J. Waterman, Schenectady; Jesse Wilson, Hampton; Mrs. S. French, Troy; E. A. Peck, Troy; Philander Curtis, Schuylerville; Miss Harriet Russell,   ; R. H. Robinson, Ballston Spa; Rev. John P. Newman, D.D., Washington, D. C.; ——— Van Valkenburgh, Ballston Spa; H. Alexander, Albany.

[2] Discourses were delivered by the Revs. Daniel Steel, D.D., Lynn, Mass.; Hiram Eddy, D.D., Jersey City; Edgar M. Levy, D.D., Philadelphia; G. L. Taylor, D.D., New Rochelle; S. H. Platt, Brooklyn; John P. Newman, D.D., Washington, D.

were not less than ten thousand. From six to eight hundred vehicles entered the gates. The temperance meetings on Monday and Tuesday were largely attended. Addresses were made by the Rev. Bishop Gilbert Haven, D.D , of Atlanta, Ga.; Rev. S. McKean, of Fort Edward; Rev. S. H. Platt, of Brooklyn; —— Johnson, of Brooklyn; Mrs. Annie Wittenmyer, of Philadelphia; Miss M. E. Winslow and Miss Lottie Coffin, of Brooklyn. The services of the meeting ended on Thursday evening, July 18th.

HON. GEORGE WEST'S COTTAGE.

FROM THE FIRST SUNDAY-SCHOOL ASSEMBLY TO THE GOSPEL TEMPERANCE MEETING, 1877-1878.

The first Sunday-School Assembly held on the grounds began its interesting sessions on Friday afternoon, July 22d, 1877, with from

C.; J. M. King, D.D., New York City; G. Hughes, Philadelphia; E. P. Hammond,   ;   C. C. McCabe, New York; A. B. Earle,   ; A. C. Rose, Stillwater; B. M. Adams, Brooklyn; C. H. Fowler, D.D., New York City; John B. Thompson, D.D., Catskill, N. Y.; —— Phelps, Vineland, N. J.; O. H. Tiffany, D.D., New York City.

three to four hundred persons in attendance. Its varied exercises were under the direction of the Rev. Alfred Taylor, D.D., of New York City. Addresses, Bible readings, sermons, lessons, microscopic and magic lantern exhibitions, concerts and praise meetings were so felicitously embraced in the week's programme that a more enjoyable course of instruction it would seem could not have been projected.[1] A quintet from New York City, two men and three women of African descent, sang very attractively many Sunday-School hymns and songs during the sessions of the assembly. A concert, in which about a thousand persons and Holding's Cornet Band of Ballston Spa took part, terminated the exercises on Friday afternoon, July 27th.

The first services of the seventh Troy Conference camp-meeting at Round Lake were held on Tuesday evening, September 4th, 1877. The Rev. L. Marshall, Presiding Elder of the Troy District, who had charge of it, preached that evening. The Women's Foreign Missionary Society of Round Lake, of which Mrs. Joseph Hillman was president, held its annual meeting on Thursday afternoon, and was addressed by the Rev. R. Hoskins and Miss Pultz, returned missionaries from India. On Sunday, September 9th, about three thousand people were on the grounds. The discourses delivered during this eight days' meetings were mostly preached by ministers of the Troy Conference.[2] The services terminated on Tuesday September 11.

[1] Addresses were made by Revs. Alfred Taylor, D.D., New York City; Theodore L. Cuyler, D.D., Brooklyn; J. M. Freeman, D.D., New York City; Bishop Gilbert Haven, D.D., Atlanta, Ga.; —— Anderson, England; H. C. Farrar, Troy, ——; O. A. Van Lennip, New York City; Rufus Wendell, Albany; B. B. Loomis, Albany; J. F. Clymer, Glens' Falls; B. F. Leipsner, Red Bank, N. J.; W. C. Steele, Brooklyn; J. McC. Holmes, D.D., Albany; O. A. Bartholomew, Troy; Rufus W. Clark, D.D., Albany; Messrs. James H. Kellogg, Troy; —— Mairs, Schenectady; A. J. Hutton, West Troy; Prof. Starr, ——; Miss Lucy J. Rider, Poultney, Vt. Sermons were preached by the Revs. Alfred Taylor, D.D., J. M. Freeman, D.D., H. C. Farrar, L. J. Matteson, D.D., Troy. The microscopic lessons and exhibitions were by Prof. Starr.

[2] Revs. L. Marshall, Presiding Elder of the Troy District; D. W. Dayton, Presiding Elder of the Saratoga District; S. M. Williams, Cambridge; D. B. McKenzie, Hampton; George Skene, Hoosick Falls; L. S. Walker, Greenbush; S. McKean, Presiding Elder of the Cambridge District; H. D. Kimball, Canajoharie; A. F. Bailey, Schuylerville; S. McLaughlin, Amsterdam; Erastus Wentworth, D.D., Fort Edward; William Osborn, ——; Homer Eaton, Presiding Elder of the Albany District; William Taylor, California; S. W. Brown, ——; W. H. Washburn, Mechanicville; J. F. Clymer, Glens' Falls; Philip Krohn, Albany; John Anderson, evangelist.

Few of the improvements made at Round Lake attracted so much public attention and comment as those begun early in the spring of 1878. Cognizant of the fame and popular features of the fine grounds at Chautauqua, the Round Lake Camp-Meeting Association contracted with the Rev. W. W. Wythe, M.D., the designer of the highly-extolled topographical representation of the land of Palestine there, to construct one on the west side of the lake at the mouth of the brook flowing through the north part of the grounds. The miniature plot, completed in July, was about five hundred feet in length, on a scale of two and a half feet to a mile. A model of the City of Jerusalem, made by the Rev. W. W. Wythe, was exhibited near it during the summer.

A large and well-appointed hotel, three stories high, with a basement and an attic, planned by J. L. Silsbee, architect, of Syracuse, N. Y., and built by J. W. Osborn, of Albany, was erected on the east side of Simpson avenue, between George and Saratoga avenues. The entire cost of the building was $22,661.24. A tunnel arched with brick, connecting the main with the eastern part of the grounds, was constructed under the highway opposite the boat landing.

The first meeting at Round Lake in the summer of 1878 was that of the Sunday-School Assembly, under the direction of the Rev. J. H. Vincent, D.D., of New York City. He and his able co-helpers, whose methods of Sunday-School superintendence and teaching, black-board exercises, Bible-readings, lectures, and sermons delighted and instructed great numbers of children and adults, made this meeting one of special excellence and commendation.[1] The vocal and instrumental music was under the direction of Prof. S. A. Ellis, of Boston. The Prof. O. A. Van Lennip's museum of Oriental curiosities and relics, Frank Beard's chalk lessons, Professor Starr's

---

[1] The following persons assisted the Rev. J. H. Vincent, D.D.: Rev. Rufus Clark, D.D., Albany; Prof. W. C. Wilkinson, Rochester Theological Seminary; Rev. J. A. Worden, secretary of the Sunday School department of the Presbyterian Church, Philadelphia; Rev. L. T. Townsend, Boston; Frank Beard, New York City; Anson Green, D.D., Toronto, Canada; J. M. King, D.D., ———; Prof. C. B. Stout, New Brunswick, N. J.; Rev. George Skene, Hoosick Falls; Rev. William Irvin, D.D., Troy; Rev. T. De Witt Talmage, D.D., Brooklyn; D. R. Niver, Albany; James H. Kelogg, Troy; J F. Clymer, Albany; B. B. Loomis, Plattsburgh; Mrs. John P. Newman, New York City; Clark Wilson and wife, ———; Rev. J. A. Worden, Rev. W. H. Boole, D.D., New York City; Rev. Edward Eggleston, D.D., Brooklyn; Rev. P. A. Chadbourne, D.D., President of Williams College, Williamstown; Rev. John P. Newman, D.D., New York City; Prof. E. Warren Clark, ———; Rev. B. K. Pierce, D.D., Boston; John E. Searles, jr., New Haven, Conn.; Rev. C. H. Fowler, D.D., LL.D., ———; George H. Thompson, Troy.

microscopic exhibitions, the singing of the Rev. Clark Wilson and his wife were also enjoyed and appreciated. The daily issue of the *Little People's Paper*, edited by the Rev. George Skene, was also popular.

A correspondent of a well-known religious journal made the following observations respecting the varied exercises: "On looking over the programme, the wonder is how all this could be covered in eight days. The wonder is no less to those who were there. But it was done, and that with a breadth and thoroughness that was scarcely less than marvelous—not only the two hours a day in the normal classes, but three lectures a day at the platform, and three conferences a day in the section tents, with two lectures a day at the Palestine park and model of the City of Jerusalem. * * *

"A Palestine park, showing the cities, rivers and sacred mountains of the Holy Land, presented the largest and finest representation of Palestine ever made, while a model of Jerusalem did the same for that city. A personal examination of these, with the lectures given, fixed them more clearly in the mind than could anything else, except a visit to the land itself. Indeed, a lady of eminence, who had traveled over Palestine, said that she had never received so clear a general impression of it as she did by these representations."[1] Fifty-five of the sixty-two persons examined on the subjects of the course of instruction of the second Round Lake Sunday-School Assembly received diplomas on Thursday, July 25th. On the afternoon of that day, the Round Lake Sunday-School Alumni Association was organized. George B. Thompson, of Troy, N. Y., was elected president, and the Rev. George Skene, secretary. On Friday morning, a short, farewell service closed the varied exercises of the assembly.

The second Union Evangelistic meeting, conducted by the Revs. E. P. Hammond, A. B. Earle and C. C. McCabe, was begun on Tuesday evening, July 30th. The noted evangelists were assisted by a number of distinguished divines of the different churches. On Friday afternoon, August 2d, the Woman's Foreign Missionary Society held its annual meeting. Miss Fannie Sparks, of the India Mission, and the Rev. John P. Newman, of New York City, addressed the society. The pathetic singing of Charles Hale, a blind boy, and the heart-cheering and soul-stirring hymns of the Rev. Clark Wilson and wife were enjoyable features of the seven days' services.

---

[1] Cor. *Presbyterian at Work.*

FROM THE GOSPEL TEMPERANCE MEETING TO THE SIXTH SUNDAY-SCHOOL ASSEMBLY, 1878-1882.

The Gospel Temperance Meeting held at Round Lake from August 6th to August 17th, 1878, drew there the largest number of people interested in the cause of temperance ever known to have assembled in one place. On four different days, upwards of ten thousand, it was estimated, were on the grounds. And on no day were there less than four thousand. Francis Murphy, the renowned reformer and apostle of temperance, who had the direction of the meeting, evoked no little of the enthusiasm which made it so remarkable in its results. He and his zealous co-workers by their persuasive and practical speeches and personal experiences incited more than four thousand persons to take pledges of total abstinence from drinking spirituous liquors, and to wear the blue ribbon badge attesting their determination to keep their promises.[1] Prof. S. A. Ellis, of Boston, conducted the singing of a choir of fifty voices. The meeting closed on Sunday evening, August 17th.

The sessions of the third Round Lake Sunday-School Assembly, conducted by the Rev. J. S. Ostrander, of New York City, began on Tuesday evening, July 8th, 1879. A wide range of instruction, embracing biblical exegesis, Sunday-school methods, kindergarten and calisthenic exercises, geography of the Holy Land, Hebrew architecture and archæology, was studiously followed by large classes daily taught in different tents and buildings. A model of Herod's temple, the third one, about six feet square, covered with gold, and a model of the wilderness tabernacle, fifteen by thirty feet, were also interesting studies. There were lectures on religious and scientific subjects and several excellent sermons.[2] On the last day

---

[1] Among the number of speakers were Captain Cyrus Sturdivant, Portland, Me.; Eccles Robinson, Pittsburgh, Pa.; Gen. Robert Love, Steubenville, Ohio; Miss Frances E. Willard, Chicago; Rev. S. T. Upham, D.D., Boston; Joseph E. King, D.D., Fort Edward; Rev. H. S. Rankin, D.D., Elmira; Frank Brady, Philadelphia; Rev. John W. Mears, D.D., Hamilton College; Col. Luther Caldwell, Elmira; Rev. S. McKean, Fort Edward; William Maxwell, Elmira; L. E. Griffith, Troy; George W. Sweet, Troy; George H. Stewart, Waterford; James Folsom, New Berlin; O. A. Brown, Gloversville; John C. Blair, Troy; H. W. Mundy, Brooklyn; Rev. H. C. Farrar, Troy.

[2] The lectures were by the Revs. William Hayes Ward, D.D., New York City; A. F. Bailey, Dalton, Mass.; D. W. Gates, Glens' Falls; John P. Newman, D.D., New York City; H. C. Farrar, Gloversville; George Skene, Troy; J. E. King, D.D., Fort Edward; J. E. C. Sawyer, Albany; B. B. Loomis, Plattsburgh; Henry

of the assembly, Friday, July 18th, thirty-five persons received diplomas and became members of the Round Lake Sunday School Alumni Association. The vocal music was under the direction of Prof. W. Warren Bentley, of New York.

COTTAGE OF REV. JOSEPH E. KING, D.D.

Darling, D.D., Albany; D. M. Reeves, D.D., Albany; M. D. Jump, Lansingburgh; J. M. King, D.D., New York City; F. Widmer, Pittsfield, Mass.

On Sunday, July 13th, sermons were delivered by the Revs. E. Wentworth, D.D., Sandy Hill; ——— Cushing, ———.

Miss Jennie B. Merrill, professor of methods in New York College, had charge of the primary work, Miss Helena L. Davis, of New York City, kindergarten instructor; and Miss Clara B. Sargent, of New York City, calisthenics.

The eighth Troy Conference camp-meeting, conducted by the Rev. S. McKean, D.D , Presiding Elder of the Cambridge District, began on Tuesday evening, July 22d, 1879. The Rev. R. H. Robinson, of Greenbush, preached that evening. Twenty-five other discourses were preached on the nine succeeding days of this interesting meeting. It closed with a sacramental service on Thursday evening, July 31st.

The Woman's National Temperance Union held its sessions on the grounds from Thursday evening, August 19th, to August 26th, 1879. The addresses of Mrs. Anne Whittenmyer (who had charge of the meetings) and her co-workers daily attracted large numbers of people to Round Lake.[2]

The second Gospel Temperance meeting, conducted by Francis Murphy, began at Round Lake on Thursday afternoon, September 4th, and interestingly continued through the succeeding three days. Large audiences were daily present and many persons pledged themselves to abstain from the use of intoxicating liquors. Besides the speeches of the eloquent advocate of temperance, those of his son and associates were enthusiastic and convincing.

The forty-sixth camp-meeting of the National Camp-Meeting Association for the promotion of holiness attracted to Round Lake

---

[1] They were preached by the Revs. J. M. Edgerton, Bethlehem; L. N. Beaudry, Montreal, Canada; W. W. Foster, Charlton; J. W. Eaton, North Adams; E. Wentworth. D.D., Sandy Hill; D. Cronk, Whitehall; Henry Graham, Troy; B. I. Ives, Auburn; D. B. McKenzie, West Sandlake; B. F. Sharpe, Greenwich; E. A, Braman, Brunswick; Charles Fletcher, New York City; S. McLoughlin, Amsterdam; S. H. Coleman, Gloversville; G. A. Barrett, Albany; D. W. Gates. Glens' Falls; Edwin George, Clifton Park; H. C. McBride, Newark, N. J.; S. W. Clemens, Broadalbin; A. Ingalls, Granville; J. L. Atwell, Middleburgh; H. C. Farrar, Gloversville; J. E. King, D.D., Fort Edward; S. W. Edgerton, Fort Ann; George Skene, Troy

[2] The speakers were Mrs. Anne Whittenmyer, ———; Mrs. ——— Butler, ———; Mrs. ——— Post, ———, Pa.; Mrs. Johnson, Brooklyn; Mrs. ——— Courtney, ———; Mrs. Wilkins, ———, Vt ; Mrs. Letitia Youmans, Pictou, Canada; Mrs. ——— Beecher, New York City; Mrs. Mary T. Burt, ———; Mrs. ——— Hill, Newark, N. J ; Mrs. ——— Denham. ———; Mrs. ——— Percival, Poughkeepsie; Mrs. ——— Gray, Albany; Miss Anna Park, Bennington, Vt.; Miss Julia Coleman. New York City; Mrs. Stowe, New York City; Miss M. E. Winslow, New York City.

[3] Thomas E. Murphy, Eccles Robinson, Hon. Lewis E. Griffith, Troy; Joseph De Goyler, Troy; Justus Miller, Troy; Charles Wenzell; Hon. ——— Brown, Galesburgh, Ill.; the Revs. W. H. Foster, jr., Fort Edward; H. D. Kimball, Albany; S. M. Williams, Cohoes; S. McKean, D.D., Fort Edward.

in 1880 people from twenty-nine states of the Union. About a hundred of the members of the Young People's Camp-Meeting Association of Ohio, in charge of Prof. R. E. Hudson, of Alliance, Ohio, with a quartette of excellent singers, attended the ten days' services. Nearly as large a body of visitors from the city of Philadelphia, under the escort of J. D. Ware, editor of the *Carriage Monthly*, was also present. The Rev. Bishop R. S. Foster, of Boston, was of the number of distinguished ministers who preached.[1] The Rev. John S. Inskip, of Philadelphia, editor of the *Christian Standard*, had charge of the meeting, which began on Saturday afternoon, June 12th, 1880, and ended on Monday morning, June 21st.

The purpose of making the Round Lake Sunday-School assemblies as popular as those of Chautauqua was again disclosed in the selection of the instructors and in the subjects embraced in the course of study and in the series of lectures of the assembly of July, 1880. The highly-qualified and distinguished superintendent of Sunday-school work, the Rev. J. A. Worden, of Princeton, N. J., had charge of it. He was ably assisted by S. W. Clark, associate editor of *The Sunday-School Times*, the Rev. H. C. Farrar, the Rev. B. B. Loomis, the Rev. Frederick Widmer, and the Rev. B. S. Everett. The sessions of the assembly began on Tuesday evening, July 20th, and terminated on Thursday evening, July 29th. The number of people attending them exceeded five thousand on one day. The course of lectures was exceedingly interesting and instructive.[2]

The masterly treatment of the subject, "The Trial and Conviction of Christ," by the Rev. Thomas Armitage, D.D., of the Fifth

[1] Those who preached were the Revs. John S. Inskip, Philadelphia; G. D. Watson, New Albany, Ind.; John A. Wood, North Attleboro, Mass.; W. L. Gray, Port Richmond, Pa.; R. A. Caruthers, Philadelphia; J. N. Short, Stoneham, Mass.; C. Munger, Kent's Hill, Me.; J. B. Foote, Canastota, N. Y.; Bishop R. S. Foster, Boston, Mass.; Alexander McLean, Yonkers, N. Y.; Joshua Gill, South Framingham, Mass.; David Updegraff (Society of Friends), Mount Pleasant, Ohio; George Hughes, Trenton, N. J.; William McDonald, Brookline, Mass.

[2] The lectures were by the following persons: Anthony Comstock, of New York City, secretary of the Society for the Suppression of Vice, "Evil Reading"; Rev. J. A. Worden, Princeton, N. J., "John Wesley"; Rev. George Macloskie, D.D., of Princeton College, "Skulls"; Rev. P. Stryker, D.D., Saratoga Springs, "Travels in the Orient"; Rev. John P. Newman, D.D., New York City, "Religious Education the Safety of the Nation"; Rev. Arthur A. Waite, Sandy Hill, "Magic"; Rev. W. P. Breed, D.D., Philadelphia, "History of a Mirror"; Rev. Francis L. Patton, D.D., Chicago, "Doubt"; Rev. R. W. Clark, Albany, "Sunday-School Work in foreign lands"; Rev. Joseph E. King, D.D., Fort Edward, "Men and Manners."

Baptist Church of New York City, elicited the highest commendations. The first discourse embraced the consideration of the religious trial of Christ before the Jewish Sanhedrim; the second, the civil trial of Christ before Pilate by the Roman law.

The crayon lessons of the Rev. Arthur A. Waite were admirable and impressive. The Sunday and other day sermons were excellent.[1] On Thursday morning, July 29th, the Round Lake Alumni Association held its annual meeting. The following persons were elected officers for 1880–1: Rev. M. D. Jump, president; George B. Thompson, vice-president; S. Palmer, secretary; A. R. Moore, treasurer. In the afternoon twenty-six graduates received diplomas.

COTTAGE OF REV. H. C. FARRAR, D.D.

[1] The sermons were by the following: Rev. Thomas Armitage, D.D., New York; Rev. J. F. Yates, Albany; Rev. Joseph E. King, D.D., Fort Edward; Rev. J. A. Worden, Princeton, N. J.; Rev. A. A. Hodge, D.D., LL.D., Princeton, N. J.

The meeting of the Woman's National Christian Temperance Union, under the direction of Miss Frances E. Willard, of Chicago, was held on the grounds in August. The opening exercises on Wednesday evening, August 11th, were conducted by Mrs. Mary C. Johnson, of Brooklyn. Mrs. Letitia Youmans, of Pictou, Canada, and other earnest advocates of temperance delivered addresses.[1] The meeting closed on Sunday evening, August 15th.

The thirteenth Troy Conference camp-meeting, held at Round Lake from Wednesday evening, September 1st, 1880, to Friday morning, September 10th, was conducted by the Rev. T. A. Griffin, Presiding Elder of the Saratoga District. The presence of seventy-six Methodist and other denominational ministers on the grounds during the meeting was a gratifying indication of the wide interest taken in the services of the annual camp-meetings held at Round Lake.[2]

The Round Lake Sunday School Assembly of 1881 was no less notable for thorough work and interesting lectures than the preceding assemblies. The zealous instructors were not only highly qualified as biblical scholars, but were admirably fitted to impart with terseness the knowledge of the subjects studied in the departments assigned them. The chief chairs of instruction were filled by the Revs. H. C. Farrar, B. B. Loomis, George Skene, Frederick Widmer, and M. D. Jump. They were assisted by the Revs. Henry D. Kimball, W. H. Washburne, S. McLaughlin, A. J. Ingalls, D. W. Gates, S. M. Williams and Prof. H. A. Wilson. Illustrated lessons on the blackboard were daily sketched by H. J. Rock, of Plattsburgh. Thirteen excellent lectures were embraced in the course. The Sunday services included three noteworthy sermons.[3] The opening

[1] Among the number of women who made addresses were Mrs. Mary T. Lathrop, of Detroit; Mrs Beecher, of Newark; Miss E. W. Greenwood, of Brooklyn; Mrs. C. C. Alford, New York; Mrs. F. G. Hibbard, of Clifton Springs; Mrs. M. F. Burt, of Brooklyn; Miss Esther Pugh, of New York; Mrs. Annie Wittenmeyer, of Philadelphia; Mrs. J. Ellen Foster, of Clinton, Iowa; Mrs. Mary R. Denham.

[2] Sermons were preached by the following ministers: Revs. A. J. Ingalls, Granville; H. C. Farrar, Gloversville; E. Wentworth, D.D., Sandy Hill; B. I. Ives, Auburn; Samuel McKean, D.D., Fort Edward; T. C. Potter, Mechanicville; Henry Graham, Troy; J. E. Russum, Adamsville; Joel W. Eaton, Lansingburgh; G. A. Barrett, Albany; S. McLaughlin, North Adams, Mass.

[3] The lectures were by the Rev. Samuel McKean, D.D., North Adams, Mass., "The Relation of Religious Truth to Mental Development"; Rev. Homer Eaton, D.D., Saratoga Springs, "California and the Yosemite"; Rev. George W. Brown, Fort Plain, "Boys"; Rev. Frederick Widmer, Lansingburgh, "Creation"; Prof.

services on Wednesday evening, July 6th, 1881, were conducted by the Rev. Frederick Widmer, Presiding Elder of the Troy District. On Saturday afternoon, July 9th, the Round Lake Branch of the Chautauqua Literary and Scientific Circle was organized. The sessions of this the fifth Round Lake Sunday-School Assembly ended on Tuesday afternoon, July 12th.

The National Camp-Meeting Association began the first services of its meeting at Round Lake in 1881 on Tuesday evening, July 12th. The initial sermon was delivered by the Rev. John S. Inskip on Wednesday morning. The subjects of the sermons of the distinguished ministers who preached were connected with that of personal holiness. The cogent arguments of these discourses and the peculiar treatment of them greatly animated the thought and feeling of the large audiences gathered daily and nightly in the auditorium.[1] The meeting closed on Thursday morning, July 21st.

The Rev. Frederick Widmer, Presiding Elder of the Troy District, conducted the fourteenth Troy Conference camp-meeting, which began on Friday evening, July 22d, 1881, and closed on Monday, August 1st. This meeting was richly blessed, and many converts accepted Christ as their Saviour.[2]

J. B. Armstrong, Poultney, Vt., Scientific; Rev. B. Hawley, D.D., Saratoga Springs, " Man and his Social Ties"; Rev. J. E. C. Sawyer, Albany, "Savonarola"; Rev. Henry Graham, Troy, " Young Men "; Rev. Daniel Dorchester, D.D., Natick, Mass., " Religious Progress"; Rev. C. W. Bennett, D.D., Syracuse University, " Typical Cities of the New Testament "; Rev. J. M. Buckley, D.D., New York City, " The Science and Art of Questioning "; Rev. E. Wentworth, D.D., Sandy Hill, " The Chinese Language "; Rev. John Humpstone, Albany, " Chrysostom "; Rev. Merritt Hulburd, Burlington, Vt., " The Dynamics of the Sunday-School Institute."

The sermons preached were by the Rev. J. M. Buckley, D.D., editor of "Christian Advocate"; Rev. Daniel Dorchester, D.D., Rev. C. W. Bennett, D.D.

[1] The sermons were preached by the Revs. John S. Inskip, Philadelphia; W. L. Gray, Philadelphia; J. A. Wood, ———; J. E. Searles, Bridgeport, Conn.; W. McDonald, Brookline, Mass.; I. Simmons, Brooklyn; B. W. Gorham, ———; R. A. Caruthers, Philadelphia; ——— Bray, ———; C. S. Uzzell, Golden, Col.; D. J. Griffin, ——— Mass.; J. N. Short, Stoneham, Mass.; ——— Morse, Putnam, Mass.; William Taylor, ———, Cal.

[2] The ministers who preached were the Revs. Frederick Widmer, Lansingburgh; C. Edwards, Whitehall; D. B. McKenzie, Crescent; J. Bridgeford, Shushan; Damas Brough, Fonda; R. H. Robinson, Greenbush; G. W. Easton, Maltaville; E. Genge, Clifton Park; J. M. Edgerton, Waterford; George Skene, Troy; H. A. Starks, Fort Edward; J. L. Humphreys, India; L. S. Walker, Sandy Hill; D. W. Gates, West Troy; S. McLaughlin, Glens' Falls; Samuel McKean, D.D., North

The Gospel Temperance meeting held on the grounds from Thursday evening, September 8th, 1881, to Sunday evening, September 11th, was largely attended by persons who had abandoned the use of intoxicating liquors. About one hundred and fifty pledges of total abstinence were taken during the meeting.[1]

The services of the National Holiness Convention organized at Round Lake on Tuesday morning, July 4th, 1882, the Rev. J. S. Inskip, president, were attended by persons from all parts of the United States, and by some from Canada, England, India, and the West Indies. The sessions of the convention closed on Wednesday night, July 5th.[2]

The annual meetings of the National Camp-Meeting Association at Round Lake were always well, if not largely, attended, and few of the ministers who preached failed to edify their hearers and to impress upon their minds the importance of holiness, which was the subject generally discoursed upon in the three sermons daily heard in the auditorium. The meeting of 1882 began on Thursday morning, July 6th, and ended on Thursday night, July 13th. Some of the ministers taking part in the services were from distant states in the South and West.

From the Sixth Sunday-School Assembly to the First Summer School, 1882–1886.

The Board of Instruction of the sixth Round Lake Sunday-School Assembly, in July, 1882, was the same as that of the assembly of Adams; I. C. Fenton, West Troy; J. G. Fallon, Troy; Miss Elizabeth Delavan, ———; Revs. C. V. Grismer, Gansevoort; J. H. Robinson, Fort Ann; Joseph E. King, D D., Fort Edward.

[1] The principal speakers were Mrs. Letitia Youmans, of Pictou, Canada; Mrs. J. Ellen Foster, of Clifton, Iowa; Col. Luther Caldwell, Elmira, and Hon. L. E. Griffith, Troy.

[2] The principal speakers were the Revs. John S. Inskip, Philadelphia; William McDonald, Brookline, Mass.; William Taylor, San Francisco, Cal.; J. A. Watson, D.D., Philadelphia.

[3] Discourses were delivered by the Revs. J. S. Inskip, Philadelphia; J. A. Wood, S. H. Henderson, Hastings, Neb.; William Jones, D.D., Lawrence, Kan.; George Prindle, ———, Iowa; J. A. Watson, D D., Philadelphia; C. Munger, Fayette, Me.; J. B Foote, Jamesville, N. Y.; ——— Haney, ———; William McDonald, ———; J. N. Short, Cambridge, Mass.; A. J. Jarrall, ———, Georgia; R. T. Kent, Griffin, Ga.; G. H. Pattello, ———, Ga.; J. E. Searles, New York; J. W. Brindell, Manchester, Iowa; A. McLean, Newburgh, N. Y.; E. M. Levy, D.D., Philadelphia; William Taylor, ———, Cal.

1881. The Rev. Frederick Widmer was general superintendent, the Rev George Skene instructor of the primary class, the Rev. H. C. Farrar of the normal, the Rev. B. B. Loomis of the post-graduate, and the Rev. M. D. Jump conductor of the conferences. H. J. Rock illustrated the lessons on the blackboard. Nearly one hundred children attended the primary course of instruction; seventy persons pursued studies in the normal department, and about forty

PERRIN W. CONVERSE'S COTTAGE.

in the post-graduate. Each of the instructors read carefully-prepared papers on the subjects studied by their classes. A series of admirable and instructive lectures was delivered by different clergymen and educated men in the auditorium.[1] The first services

[1] The lectures were by the following persons : Rev. H. A. Starks, Fort Edward, "Culture"; Rev. Joel W. Eaton, D.D., Lansingburgh, "Russia and the Greek Church"; Rev. Elam Marsh, Argyle, "John the Baptist"; Rev. H. M. King, D.D., Albany, "Africa, past and present"; Rev. William H. Hughes, Schenectady, "Moral Dwarfs"; Mr. S. C. Hutchins, Albany, "The Newspaper and Civilization"; Prof. Edward H. Rice, Pittsfield, "David and his Scholars"; Attarian Effendi, Armenia, "The People of Turkey"; Rev. S. V. Leech, D D., Albany, "The Perils of Genius"; Rev. G. S. Chadbourne, Cambridge, Mass., "Your Work"; Prof. C. V. D. Connell, Millport. N. Y., "The Interim"; Rev. J. W. Thompson, Greenbush, "Illusions and Mistakes"; Rev. Henry A. Cordo, D.D., Gloversville, "The Sunday-School Ideal"; Rev. William J. Heath, Cohoes, "Music and its Uses"; Rev. J. E. C. Sawyer, Albany, "Right Royal"; Rev.

of prayer and praise were held on Wednesday evening, July 19th. The sessions of the assembly closed on Friday, July 28th. On the last day of the assembly the Rev. H. C. Farrar suggested the need of a building for the use of the alumni, and urged the erection of one on the grounds. Eleazer A. Peck, of Troy, to further the undertaking, generously gave two of his lots at Round Lake as a subscription.

An enjoyable event of the summer of 1882 was the presentation of the oratorio of "Joseph" on Thursday evening, August 10th, in the auditorium. About sixty singers, under the direction of Prof. C. G. Norris, of Troy, rendered the different parts of the sacred composition.

The introductory services of the fifteenth Troy Conference camp-meeting at Round Lake, conducted by the Rev. J. E. C. Sawyer, Presiding Elder of the Albany District, on Tuesday evening, August 15th, 1882, were the devotional exercises of prayer and praise common to the first meeting day. Daily thereafter three sermons were usually preached; the audiences numbering from five hundred to two thousand people.[1] The meeting closed on Friday morning, August 25th, with a service of prayer and praise.

The Gospel Temperance meeting, conducted by the Rev. Samuel McKean, D.D., of North Adams, Mass., assisted by the Rev. H. C. Farrar, of Troy, N. Y., began on Thursday afternoon, September 7th, 1882, and closed on the following Sunday evening. Rev. and

Henry Gordon, D.D., Colla, "Divine Revelation a necessity"; Attarian Effendi, "Life in Turkey"; Rev. Henry D. Kimball, New Bedford, Mass., "Henry of Navarre"; Prof. F. W. Stowell, Gloversville, "The Creative Week"; Rev. J. H. Griffith, D.D., Troy, "Power of Character."

Prof. H. A. Williams, of Albany, gave a series of readings, and Prof. H. A. Wilson, of Saratoga Springs, lectured on the Holy Land at Palestine Park.

The sermons preached were by the Revs. George S. Chadbourne and S. V. Leech, D.D.

[1] The following ministers preached sermons: Revs. C. W. Rowley, East Greenbush; W. J. Chapman, Sprout Brook; L. S. Walker, Castleton; W. J. Heath, Cohoes; F. Wilson, Hudson; B. K. Pierce, D.D., Boston; E. Wentworth, D.D., Sandy Hill; T. G. Thompson, D.D., Kinderhook; S V. Leech, D.D., Albany; G. W. Brown, Saratoga Springs; J. W. Thompson, Greenbush; J. E. C. Sawyer, Albany; D. W. Gates, Albany; R. H. Robinson, West Troy; E. Genge, Green Island; J. H. Robinson, Fort Ann; E. McChesney, Troy; G. A. Barrett, Ballston Spa; Samuel McKean, D.D., North Adams, Mass.; William M. Bundage, Ames, N. Y.; Bostwick Hawley, D.D., Saratoga Springs; Alfred Eaton, Wilton; Merritt Hulburd Burlington, Vt.; J. H. Coleman, Albany; S. M. Williams, Valley Falls.

Mrs. Clark Wilson, of Towanda, Pa., were the chief singers. A number of excellent addresses on temperance was delivered by prominent clergymen and other advocates of total abstinence.[1]

No meetings were held on the grounds during the year 1883. The association had become financially embarrassed by unremuner-

CHARLES D. HAMMOND'S COTTAGE.

[1] Rev. John P. Newman, New York, "Attitudes of temperance to the political issues of the day"; Rev. S. V. Leech, Albany, "The battle for prohibition in the Empire State"; Henry C. Bascom, Troy, "Relations of diet to drunkenness"; Rev. H. C. Farrar, Troy, poem; Rev. G. H. Corey, Tarrytown, address; Charles Wenzell, West Troy; Rev. D. W. Dayton, Amsterdam.

ative improvements, and was for a time unable to adjust its affairs acceptably to its creditors. Fortunately, the efforts and contributions of the officers, lot-owners, and friends of the association were the means of lessening its liabilities and of reducing its debt. A resolution was passed at the meeting of the trustees on February 2d, 1884, thanking the late bondholders for their generous concessions and the friends of the association who had wholly or in part surrendered the bonds held by them or who had made subscriptions whereby the indebtedness of the association was reduced from $98,000 to $25,000.

The first of the three meetings held on the grounds in 1884, was the Round Lake Sunday-School Assembly, which began its sessions with a vesper service on Tuesday evening, July 15th. The Rev. H. C. Farrar was the instructor of the normal class, the Rev. B. B. Loomis of the post-graduate, and the Rev. George Skene of the primary. The kindergarten was in charge of Mrs. Helena D. Van Denburg. Elocution was taught by Miss Anna H. Lancashire, and painting and clay modeling by Miss Ida H. Pulis. Crayon lessons on the blackboard were given by H. J. Rock. Prof. A. E. Decker conducted the singing, and Miss Anna Loomis was organist. The course of instruction embraced many new subjects of study and discussion, and the series of daily lectures was highly appreciated. [1]

[1] The subjects of the lectures were : "The importance of special work for young men," by Rev. T. G. Darling, Schenectady; "The necessity for the Young Men's Christian Association," by Rev. Charles W. Cushing, D.D., Rochester; "Tying and Tied," by Rev. Ellis S. Osborne, D.D., Kingston; "Charles H. Spurgeon," by Rev. Henry M. King, D.D., Albany; "One-third of a man," by Rev. E. D. Huntley, D.D., Washington, D. C.; "Should the education the American college gives be wholly religious?" by Rev. Henry Darling, D.D., Hamilton College; "The church of the future as our educator," by Rev. C. N. Sims, D.D., LL.D., Chancellor of Syracuse University; "The air, its chemical properties and physical qualities," by Prof. William W. McGilton, Fort Edward; "The Bible among the sacred books," by Rev. Ensign McChesney, Ph.D., Troy; "A budget of blunders," by Rev. M. D. Jump, Burlington, Vt.; "Mexico," by Rev. William Butler, D.D, India; "North America evangelized—the evangelizer of the world," by Rev. C. P. Sheldon, D.D., Troy; "The missionary spirit of the Sunday-School," by James H. Kellogg, Troy; "Bible customs and manners," by Attarian Effendi, Armenia; "Bible astronomy," by R. C. Clark, Whitehall; "The book we study," by Rev. R. R. Meredith, D.D., Boston; "Paris," by Rev. James M. King, D.D., New York City; "Webster, Irving and Mrs. Browning as models for students," by Rev. S. V. Leech, D.D., Albany; "God in history," by Rev. E. P. Stevens, Hoosick Falls; "Money and morals," by Hon. H. G. Coggeshall, Waterville, N. Y.

The Sunday sermons were delivered by the Rev. William Butler, D.D., Missionary from India, and the Rev. E. D. Huntley, D.D., of Washington, D. C.

Wednesday, July 16th, was denominated the Young Men's Christian Association Day; Friday, July 18th, College Day; Monday, July 21st, Missionary Day; Wednesday, July 23d, Chautauqua Literary and Scientific Circle Day; Thursday, July 24th, Commencement Day. Special exercises marked each of the days.

On Friday afternoon, July 18th, Alumni Hall, on the south side of Whitfield Avenue, was dedicated. The erection of the building was begun in April, and in June it was completed, at a cost of $1,900; the money having been contributed by the alumni and the friends of the Round Lake Alumni Association. The dedicatory exercises at the Auditorium included an address by the zealous projector and earnest supporter of the undertaking, the Rev. H. C. Farrar, one by the Rev. William Griffin, D.D., and the reading of a dedicatory poem by the Rev. Joseph E. King, D.D., who wrote it. At Alumni Hall, a dedicatory prayer was offered by the Rev. R. H. Robinson, D.D., which was followed by the singing of the long meter doxology, and by the benediction, pronounced by the Rev. Ensign McChesney, Ph.D.

The musical and literary entertainment on Saturday evening, July 19th, was attended by more than two thousand people. On Thursday evening, July 24th, the exercises of Commencement Day concluded those of the assembly.

The first services of the sixteenth Troy Conference camp-meeting at Round Lake, on Tuesday evening, August 12th, 1884, were attended by more than six hundred persons. The Rev. J. H. Bond, Presiding Elder of the Plattsburgh District, had the direction of the services of the six days' meeting, which closed on Monday morning, August 18th, with a love-feast.[1]

The third, and last meeting of the year, was the Gospel Temperance meeting conducted by the Rev. John A. Copeland, of Lancaster, New York. It began on Tuesday afternoon, August 26th, and continued to Monday evening, September 1st. The presence and addresses of ex-Governor John P. St. John, of Kansas, the

---

[1] Sermons were preached by the following ministers: Revs. J. C. Russum, Troy; C. W. Rowley, Canajoharie; W. W. Foster, Clifton Park; H. C. Farrar, Troy; D. N. Lewis, Jonesville; S. V. Leech, D.D., Albany; Henry Graham, Gloversville; James M. King, D.D., New York; A. D. Heaxt, Westport; L. Marshall, Johnstown; T. G. Thompson, Granville; P. L. Dow, Quaker Springs; Joseph E. King, D.D., Fort Edward; I. N. Beaudry, Montreal; —— Colman (Baptist), Bridgeport, Conn.

presidential candidate of the Prohibition party, gave considerable fame to the meeting.[1]

A most enjoyable occasion was the Grand Army and Chaplains' Reunion at Round Lake, under the direction of Colonel G. A. Cantine, of Rome, N. Y., post department inspector. The Albany City Band furnished the instrumental music. On Thursday morning, September 4th, the two days' meeting was inaugurated by an address of welcome delivered by Col. G. A. Cantine, which was responded to by the Rev. E. L. Allen, D.D., of Highland, N, Y., department chaplain of the Grand Army of the Republic. The posts of Troy, Albany, Cohoes, West Troy, Argyle, Schenectady and the other neighboring places were largely represented. On Friday afternoon, Col. Frederick D. Grant came from Mount McGregor, bringing

M. B. SHERMAN'S COTTAGE.

from his sick father " cordial greetings to the old soldiers " meeting at Round Lake, of whom there were about three thousand on the

[1] The other prominent speakers were Mrs. Laura G. Faxon, of Albert Lee, Minn.; Mrs. Letitia Youmans, Canada; Mrs. Mary T. Lathrop, Detroit; Rev. Daniel Dorchester, D.D., Natick, Mass.; Mrs. C. H. St. John, Denver, Col.; Mrs. W. H. Boole, Brooklyn; ex-Gov. John P. St. John; Rev. W. H. Boole, Brooklyn.

grounds. That afternoon, the Rev. John P. Newman, D.D., of New York City, eloquently spoke on "the Civil War and its results." The interesting exercises of the afternoon terminated the meeting.

The Round Lake Sunday-School Assembly of 1885 greatly advanced the fame of the chief instructors who, with much painstaking and zeal, acquitted themselves of their respective duties in the departments of which they had charge. The instruction of the post-graduate class was assigned to the Rev. H. C. Farrar, and that of the normal class to the Rev. B. B. Loomis. Miss Stella M. King had charge of the boys and girls' department, Miss Helena C. Augustine of the kindergarten, and Miss Martha Van Marter of the primary conferences. Miss Eliza M. Clark taught drawing, Mrs. Frank J. Harris painting, Mrs. M. F. Biscoe elocution, Mrs. K. J. Boughton clay modeling, M. A. Walter phonography, and Edward Marsh penmanship. Prof. J. E. Van Olinda was musical director and Miss Clara Stearns pianist. The long session of fourteen days, beginning on Tuesday evening, July 14th, and ending on Monday evening, July 27th, was made exceedingly interesting by profitable and enjoyable courses of study, musical and literary entertainments, and a large number of lectures on many important subjects.[1] A

[1] The subjects of the lectures were the following: "Work and Workers," "Materialism and the Microscope," by Rev. D. H. Snowdon, Ph.D., Ill.; "An Old Castle," "College Education," by Prof. T. C. Winchester, of Wesleyan University; "Natural Law in the Spirit World," by Rev. J. Zweifel, Whitehall; "Elijah," an epic poem, by Rev. George Lansing Taylor, D.D., Brooklyn; "English Literature and Culture," "Rise and Decline of the English Drama and the Growth of Prose," "Milton and the Poetry of the Nineteenth Century," "Some Literary Londoners of the Eighteenth Century," by Prof. William E. Mead, Troy; "The Story of a piece of Sandstone, Coal and Marble," by Prof. W. W. McGilton, Fort Edward; "Among the Glaciers of the High Alps," by Rev. I. J. Lansing, New York; "The Pyramids," "The Tabernacle," by Rev. H. A. Starks, Albany; "Historic Art," by J. L. Corning, D.D., Terre Haute, Ind.; "The Christology of the Bible," by Rev. C. F. Burdick, Valley Falls; "Crime and its Shadows," by Rev. Silas Edgerton, chaplain of Sing Sing prison; "Beauty," by Eugene Bouton, Albany; "The Bible in the Light of Recent Discoveries in Oriental Lands," by Rev. John P. Newman, D.D., New York; "Progress of Doctrine in the New Testament," by Rev. T. G. Thompson, Granville; "Divorce, its Causes and Effects," "The Family as an American Institution," "The Divorce Question in the Light of Modern Civilization," by Rev. Samuel W. Dike, Royalton, Vt.; "Old Catacombs," by Rev. W. H. Withrow, D.D., Toronto, Canada; "Paul at Athens," by Rev. W. W. Foster, jr., Albany; "The Uses of Ugliness," by Rev. Jahu DeWitt Miller, Philadelphia; "The Industrial Policy of England," by E. A. Hartshorn, Troy; "Plato and John, the Apostle, Compared," by Rev. H. A. Buttz, D.D., Madison, N. J.; "The Word Within the Word," by Rev. A. D. Vail, D.D., New York; "Old Clothes,"

model of the Tabernacle and a half-section of the Great Pyramid, in miniature, were erected near Alumni Hall, and were the subjects of several lectures. On Sunday, July 19th, the new auditorium was dedicated by the Rev. John P. Newman, D.D. The building, 104 by 80 feet, erected at a cost of $3,152 18, was furnished with sittings for two thousand people. The two concerts of vocal and instrumental music, conducted by Prof. J. E. Van Olinda, were enjoyed by large audiences. The exercises on C. L. S. C. Day, July 21st,[1]

JOHN D. ROGERS' COTTAGE.

by A. L. Blair, Saratoga Springs; "Cross Wives," by Rev. V. M. Simmons, Springfield, Mass.; "The New Testament Missionary Work," by Rev. J. E. C. Sawyer, Troy.

The sermons were preached by the Rev. H. A. Buttz, D.D., president of Drew Theological Seminary, Rev. John P. Newman, D.D., Rev. I. J. Lansing, and by Rev. Edwin F. See, Albany.

On Missionary Day addresses were made by the Rev. N. G. Clark, secretary of the A. B. C. F. M., and by Chaplain C. C. McCabe, secretary of the Missionary Society.

[1] On C. L. S. C. Day the Rev. John H. Vincent, D.D., New York, delivered an address.

and on Sunday, July 26th, Young Men's Christian Association Day, were made very interesting.[1]

The Troy Conference camp-meeting, conducted by the Rev. Homer Eaton, D.D., Presiding Elder of the Cambridge District, began on Tuesday evening, August 11th, 1885, and closed Thursday morning, August 20th. The attendance was uniformly good, and the sermons practical and impressive.[2]

The five days denominated "The Oriental Week," beginning July 1st and ending July 5th, 1886, were devoted to such representations, entertainments, and exercises as contributed information respecting the manners and customs of the people of the East. Mrs. John P. Newman, of Washington, D. C., who had accompanied her distinguished husband in making a tour of the world, and had collected in Eastern countries many valuable and interesting mementoes of places visited by them, having admirably planned the services, tableaux and exhibitions, was highly complimented for making them so attractive and instructive.

On Thursday morning, July 1st, at ten o'clock, Peter Von Finkelstein, a native of Jerusalem, dressed as a Mohammedan muezzin, cried the hour of prayer from the bell-tower of the auditorium, when services of praise and prayer held in a number of cottages inaugurated the exercises of the "Opening Day," which in part embraced the reading of the Holy Scriptures in English, Arabic, Urdu, Hindoostanee and other languages, and also the singing of hymns in several languages spoken by people of the Orient. The illustrated lectures, the costume tableaux, and the musical and literary entertainments were very enjoyable. The Rev. John P. Newman, D.D., on Sunday, July 4th, preached a sermon in the morning, and in the evening Peter Von Finkelstein, delivered a

---

[1] On Young Men's Christian Association Day, Sunday, July 26th, the speakers were Rev. George A. Hall, State Sec.; F. S. Wetherbee, Port Henry; Charles S. Judd, J. B. Rogers, Rev. H. A. Starks, F. W. Ober and D. A. Budge.

[2] The sermons were preached by the Revs. C. M. Clark, Schoharie; D. R. Lowell, Albany; J. C. Russum, Troy; L. A. Dibble, Shelborne, Vt.; J. W. Bennett, Presiding Elder of the Burlington District; Henry Graham, D.D., Troy; Rev. John P. Newman, D.D., New York; E. H. Brown, Troy; C. R. Hawley, Troy; H. N. Munger, Esperance, ———; M. D. Jump, Burlington, Vt.; J. Zweifel, Whitehall; G. W. Brown, Fonda; H. S. Rowe, Galway; S. M. Adsit, Charlton; C. W. Rowley, D.D., Canajoharie; G. W. Barrett, Schenectady; J. O. Knowles, D.D., Boston; J. W. Hamilton, D.D., Boston; J. H. Coleman, Gloversville; Bishop Wiliard F. Mallalieu, New Orleans; T. A. Griffin, Greenbush.

lecture on the religious aspects of the East. Many sacred hymns and songs were charmingly sung by Mrs. Joseph F. Knapp, of Brooklyn, and Miss Anna Budden, of Pithoragarh, India, read selections of prose and poetry at the evening entertainments. On Monday evening, July 5th, there was a brilliant display of fireworks at Prospect Park, near the lake.

From the First Summer School to the First Round Lake Meeting, 1886.

The establishment of a Summer School at Round Lake in 1886 deserved the success which attended it. Wisely planned to afford all the educational advantages which other institutions of its kind offered, and to excel them by opening many pleasurable paths of learning by new methods of instruction and illustration, the school readily secured the position and favor which its sagacious projectors desired for it. The chairs of the different departments of instruction were filled by experienced teachers representing some of the principal universities, colleges, and institutions of learning. History, mathematics, economics, psychology, physiology, zoology, botany, geology, astronomy, chemistry, elocution, drawing, painting, modeling, music, and other branches of knowledge, were taught. Instruction in the modern and dead languages included English, Anglo-Saxon, French, German, Spanish, Italian, Latin, Greek and Hebrew. Two or more lectures were delivered daily by distinguished scholars, scientists, and travelers. Ideal tours through Europe, conversations in German and French, geological and botanical excursions, social entertainments, vocal and instrumental concerts, readings and recitations, microscopic exhibitions were profitably enjoyed by the large body of students. James H. Worman, Ph.D., of Vanderbilt University, the eminent linguist and teacher, was the highly-qualified director of the school. The other members of the faculty were men and women of marked culture and ability.[1]

---

[1] James H. Worman, Ph.D., French, German, Spanish; Edward W. Bemis, D.D., Springfield, Mass. (of Johns Hopkins University), history and economics; Prof. I. P. Bishop, Chatham High School, Chatham, N. Y., history, geology and chemistry; Charles J. Little, LL.D., Syracuse University, psychology; Prof. A. W. Norton, Elmira, N. Y., mathematics; Prof. M. S. Bloodgood, New York, art; Prof. William R. M. French, Chicago Art Institute, lectures on art; J. H. Hoose, Ph.D., Cortland State Normal School, teaching; Prof. Alexander E. Frye, Normalville, Ill., geography and oratory; Gen. T. J. Morgan, D.D., Providence, R. I., pedagogy; Prof. W. E. Wilson, Rhode Island State Normal

The five weeks' session of the school was inaugurated on Monday evening, July 12th, by a concert conducted by Prof. J. E. Van Olinda, the director of the choral music. The different selections of music were delightfully rendered by the choir of the Second Presbyterian Church of Troy and by members of the Troy Choral Union. The school closed on Thursday, August 12th.

In 1886 each of the fifteen days of the ninth Round Lake Sunday-School Assembly's session was designated by a distinctive name. Beginning with Tuesday, July 20th, the opening day, the others were the Scientific, College, Oriental, Industrial Art, Baccalaureate, Superintendents and Teachers', Chautauqua Literary and Scientific Circle, Fine Art, Children's, Missionary, Recreation (Sunday), Alumni, and Commencement. The hours of each day were usually allotted to instruction, lectures, and meetings in the following order: 8 A. M., early morning lecture, instruction of normal, intermediate and primary classes; 10 A. M., devotions; 10.50 A. M., lecture; 1.45 P. M., conference; 2.30 P. M., lecture; 4 P. M., instruction of post-graduate and normal classes; 5 P. M., kindergarten instruction; 7 P. M., conference; 8 P. M., lecture.

The Rev. H. C. Farrar, D.D., and the Rev. B. B. Loomis, who had so admirably conducted the assembly of 1885, were given the management of the assembly of 1886. The board of instruction consisted of the Rev. B. B. Loomis, post-graduate class; the Rev. J. S. Ostrander, normal class; the Rev. H. C. Farrar, intermediate class; Mrs. J. S. Ostrander, primary class; Miss Effie M. Fraats, kindergarten; Miss Stella M. King, elocution; Prof. J. E. Van Olinda, director of music, and Miss Clara Stearns, pianist. The daily lectures were on subjects of much interest and importance, and covered a wide field of thought, investigation, and observation.[1] Be-

School, botany, physiology, zoology; Prof. T. M. Balliett, Reading, Pa., psychology; Prof. J. E. Allen, Rochester, American history; A. W. Winship, Boston, lecture on mental training; Prof. J. B. Southworth, lecture on teaching fractions; Prof. D. A. Schermerhorn, Hudson, N. Y., penmanship; Mrs. Jeanie Spring Peet, Perth Amboy, N. J., clay and sand modeling; Miss Eliza M. Clark, Troy, N. Y., industrial drawing; Miss Mary B. White, New Bedford, Mass., model school, theory and practice of teaching; Miss Bernice Long, Saratoga High School, penmanship; Miss L. A. McEntee, New York Mills, phonography and typewriting; Miss Effie J. Fraats, Albany, kindergarten; Miss Ida M. Isdell, Albany, kindergarten; Miss O. A. Evers, Manchester, N. H., model school, mathematics; Prof. A. Pégou, Boston Parisian Academy of Music, vocalization; Mme. A. Pégou, piano; Prof. J. E. Van Olinda, Troy, chorus class.

[1] The lectures were: "The Regal Power of the Teacher," by Rev. James M. King, D.D., New York; "Native Mettle," and "Landmarks of Scott," by Wallace

sides the vocal music conducted by Prof. J. E. Van Olinda, the singing of the Courtney Ladies' Quartette of New York, and of the Wyoming Trio, and the *soirée musicale* of Prof. A. and Mme. A. Pégou, of the Boston Parisian Academy of Music, assisted by Mme. H. E. Cuvellier, of Washington, D. C., and the humorous readings and recitations of Charles F. Underhill, of New York, delightfully entertained large audiences at the auditorium and Alumni Hall. On Wednesday, July 28th, the Round Lake Society of Fine Arts was organized by the election of the Rev. H. C. Farrar, D.D., president; J. H. Worman, Ph.D., vice president, Rev. B. B. Loomis, secretary and treasurer.

The session of the assembly closed on Tuesday, August 3d.

The Woman's Christian Temperance Union of Saratoga County held its third annual meeting at Round Lake on Tuesday and Wednesday, August 17th and 18th.

Bruce, Poughkeepsie; "The Practical Value of the Microscope," by R. H. Ward, M.D., Troy; "Political Economy," by Edward W. Bemis, D.D., Springfield, Mass.; "The Broader Education," by Rev. J. Harwood Pattison, D.D., Rochester; "The Scholar for the Times," by Charles J. Little, LL.D., Syracuse University; "Parliamentary Practice" (four lectures), by Rev. T. B. Neely, D.D., Pottsville, Pa.; "Egypt, Ancient and Modern," by Hon. George S. Batcheller, Saratoga Springs; "Pyramid of Ghizeh," by Rev. H. A. Starks, Albany; "Industrial Education," by Hon. Arthur MacArthur, Washington, D. C.; "Artist and Publisher," and "Art and Christian Worship," by Rev. Edward L. Hyde, Middleborough, Mass.; "Chatterton, the Boy-Poet of a Century Ago," by Rev. Albert Danker, Ph.D., Watertown; "Mosaic Era," by Hon. William H. Tefft, Whitehall; "Westminster Abbey," and "The Yellowstone," by Rev. George H. Wells, Montreal; "The Earth," by Prof. Alexander E. Frye, Normalville, Ill.; "Effects of Alcohol on Nutrition," by Prof. W. E. Wilson, Providence, R. I.; "Public Speakers and their Methods," by Rev. Samuel McKean, D.D., Lansingburgh; "The Art of Reading," by Alfred Ayres; "The Missionary Outlook," by Rev. C. C. Creegan, Syracuse; "Aggressive Christian Work," by Rev. Robert S. MacArthur, D.D., New York; "The Outlook of Foreign Missions," by Rev. I. J. Lansing, Brooklyn; "A Knapsack Tour from New York to Central India," by Rev. T. F. Clark, ———; "John and Jonathan," by Rev. Robert Nourse, Washington, D. C.; "Poets and Poetry," by Rev. G. W. Adams, ———, Pa.; "The Lost Doctrine," by H. K. Carroll, LL.D., New York; "Bible Inspiration," by Prof. W. J. Shaw, Montreal; "Bible Astronomy in the Light of Modern Science," by R. C. Cooke, Whitehall; "Possibilities and Perils of Our Country," by Rev. Jahu De Witt Miller, Philadelphia; "Court, Camp, and Church," by Rev. E. M. Mills, Ph.D., Elmira.

Sermons were preached by Bishop R. S. Foster, D.D., LL.D., Boston; Gen. Thomas J. Morgan, D.D., Providence, R. I.; Rev. Robert Nourse; Rev. E. M. Mills, Ph.D.; Prof. W. I. Shaw.

The first Round Lake meeting, conducted by the Rev. R. H. Robinson, D.D., president of the association, began on Thursday evening, August 19th, with a service of praise and prayer. The first

JOHN C. IDE'S COTTAGE.

sermon was preached by the Rev. H. C. Farrar, D.D., on the following Friday morning.[1] From Wednesday, August 25th, to the close of the meeting on Sunday night, August 29th, the noted revivalists, the Revs. Sam. Jones, of Cartersville, Ga., and Sam. Small, of Atlanta, Ga., preached with marked acceptance and power to great throngs of people, numbering from five to fifteen thousand. The singing of Prof. E. O. Excel, of Chicago, and J. Maxwell, of Cin-

---

[1] Discourses were afterward delivered by the Revs. D. F. Brooks, Ketcham's Corners; L. N. Beaudry, Montreal; L. H. King, D.D., New York; Joseph E. King, D.D., Fort Edward; D. Halloran, Newport, N. J.; P. N. Chase, Roxbury, N. Y.; J. M. Edgerton, Round Lake; Samuel Meredith, Presiding Elder of Saratoga District; J. J. Noe, Middlebury, Vt.; J. G. Fallon, Schuylerville.

cinnati, who accompanied the famous evangelists, was exceedingly impressive.

WATER-WORKS.

In the fall of 1886 plans were considered by the association for conducting more water to the grounds from the unfailing springs on the west side of the railroad, and to effect a system of sewers for the inhabited part of the property. Charles D. Hammond, M. B. Sherman, Silas Owen, E. A. Hartshorn, and the Rev. William Griffin, D.D., were appointed a commission having the superintendence and direction of the projected improvements, which were begun in April, 1887. A receiving reservoir was constructed east of the supplying springs on the wooded declivity west of the railroad. Two storage tanks, severally having a capacity of 37,000 gallons, were built on the eminence west of the pump-house on the north side of the receiving reservoir, from which water is now pumped into the tanks. Connected with the main from them, lateral pipes branching to different points were laid to supply the cottages and other buildings with water. Hydrants and drinking fountains were judiciously located about the grounds. The use of the water is available to a height of eighty feet. The work of laying the pipes and of constructing the reservoir and tanks was accomplished early in June.

The sewerage of the grounds by adequate conduits was also satisfactorily accomplished. The sanitary benefits of the system are the more appreciable, inasmuch as no sewage contaminates the water of the lake.

M. B. SHERMAN HOSE COMPANY.

The M. B. Sherman Hose Company, of Round Lake, was organized June 18th, 1887, by the election of the following officers: Charles P. Ide, president; M. L. Barnes, vice-president; Charles D. Rogers, secretary; J. F. Fellows, treasurer; A. E. Batchelder, captain; F. A. Converse, first assistant; T. N. Derby, second assistant. The company comprises thirty members. A fine hose carriage was presented to the Round Lake Association by M. B. Sherman, of Albany, one of the trustees of the association. Five hundred feet of hose were furnished the company by the association.

EVENTS OF 1887.

The opening day of the Round Lake Summer School of 1887, on Tuesday, July 12th, was auspiciously fair and pleasant. The exer-

GRIFFIN INSTITUTE.

cises at the auditorium at 10.30 A. M., attracted there an audience numbering more than two thousand people. The Citizens' Band of Ballston Spa, and the Schaghticoke Glee Club, pleasurably entertained them with instrumental and vocal music. Prof. George Prentice, of Wesleyan University, read the CXXVII. Psalm, and the Rev. Bishop Cyrus D. Foss, of Minneapolis, Minn., offered a prayer. The Rev. William Griffin, D.D., the president of the association, in a brief address adverted to the advanced position which Round Lake had taken as a seat of religious, mental and moral culture, and the gratifying evidences of its prosperity and growth. The Rev. John P. Newman, D.D., with his brilliant elocution, delivered a thoughtful address on "The moral value of education." The critical and comprehensive view taken by Gen. L. P. di Cesnola, of "The practical value of the museum," was highly instructive. The Hon. William M. Evarts made the occasion memorable by his cogent arguments and rational conclusions respecting "The national value of education." The short address by the Hon. Warner Miller, claimed by the enthusiastic audience, was one of pertinent observations on popular education. The Hon. Levi P. Morton, who, with other distinguished men, was present, although likewise solicited, politely bowed his declination to address the urgent audience. The poetical contribution, entitled "Opening Day at Round Lake," by the Rev. Joseph E. King, D.D., elicited much applause.

In the afternoon, at 4 o'clock, the Grant memorials were unveiled in the George West Museum of Art and Archæology by Mrs. John P. Newman, in the presence of a large number of persons.

At the auditorium in the evening, short speeches were made by prominent men interested in the welfare of the association. Afterward, a display of fireworks was made on the western hill.

The direction of the summer school of 1887, has been given to J. H. Worman, Ph.D., who so successfully and ably conducted the school of 1886. The departments of methods and practice, fine arts, oratory and expression, history and economics, languages, natural science, industrial art, the model primary and intermediate school and the kindergarten have accomplished and experienced teachers[1]. The four weeks' session of the school will end on August 5th.

---

[1] The instructors and lecturers engaged are J. H. Hoose, Ph.D., superintendent; I. T. Balliett, W. N. Hailmann, D.D., H. R. Sanford, A. W. Norton, Miss Mary B. White, Prof. G. Guttenberg, Prof. Alex. E. Frye, W. H. Smith, school of methods and practice; Edward W. Bemis, Ph.D., history and economics; Prof.

The Round Lake Assembly of 1887, to be conducted by the Revs. H. C. Farrar, D.D., and B. B. Loomis, Ph.D., will begin its seventeen days' session on Wednesday evening, July 20th, 1887. The faculty will be the Rev. H. C. Farrar, D.D., superintendent of instruction; Rev. B. B. Loomis, Ph.D., normal class; Rev. M. D. Jump, post-graduate class; Rev. W. H. Groat, intermediate class; Mrs. Julia Terhune, primary class; Prof. J. E. Van Olinda, musical director, and Miss Clara Stearns, pianist. The lectures will be exceedingly edifying.[1] The session of the assembly will end on August 5th.

The Round Lake meeting of 1887, to begin on August 13th, and end August 23d, will be one of the most notable in the history of the place. The great revivalists, the Revs. Sam. Jones and Sam. Small, will have charge of it and will preach daily. Prof. E. O. Excel will also be present during the ten days' meeting, and will

---

Alex. E. Frye, geography; Prof. G. Guttenberg, I. P. Bishop, Prof. Brands, natural science; I. P. Bishop, chemistry and geology; R. H. Ward, M.D., microscopy; J. H. Worman, Ph.D., Prof. E. Von Fingerlin, T. B. Chapin, James A. Harrison, Ph.D., Prof. Wm. T. Thorn, Mrs. J. H. Worman, Miss N. Colbert, Miss Bertha Kunz, Miss Ida M. Hollis, Miss E. P. Rollins, German, French, Spanish, Italian, English, Anglo-Saxon, Latin and Greek languages; William R. M. French, B. R. Fitz, Alex. E. Frye, industrial drawing; Miss Mirian W. Dowd, charcoal drawing; Miss Florence E. Jinks, crayon heads; Mrs. Jeanie S. Peet, clay modeling; Homer A. Norris, Ernest Longley, instrumental music, piano and organ; Charles E. Tinney, Mrs. Otis Rockwood and Prof. Edwin C. Rowley, vocal; W. N. Hailmann, D.D., Miss Hailmann, kindergarten; Prof. J. W. Churchill, L. T. Powers, Prof. Frank H. Fenno, oratory and expression; W. G. Anderson, M.D., Miss Marion F. Carter, physical training; Miss L. M. Morrill, book-keeping; Miss M. E. St. George, phonography and typewriting.

[1] The subjects of the lectures as published will be "Fits and Misfits," by Rev. J. W. Hamilton, D.D.; "Ready Wit," by Wallace Bruce; "Dickens' Great Characters," by Prof. Nathan Sheppard; "Our Shadows," by J. F. Clymer; "The Stranger at Our Gates," by Rev. Jahu DeWitt Miller; "Art, the Mirror of the Ages," by J. L. Corning, D.D.; "Manliness in Professional Life," by Prof. J. D. Phelps; "A Knack of Drawing," by Prof. W. M. R. French; "Egyptology," by Rev. H. A. Starks; "Strategy in Teaching," by Rev. Marcus D. Buell; "An Evening with the Pharaohs," by H. A. Starks; "Milton as an Educator," by Prof. Homer B. Sprague; "An Hour with the Caricaturists," by Prof. W. M. R. French; "What Woman has Done in Art for a Thousand Years," by J. L. Corning, D.D.; "From Boston to Bareilly and Back," by Rev. Wm. Butler, D.D.; "The Coming Religion," by Rev. Emory J. Haynes, D.D.; "Our Boys and Girls," by Rev. Thomas Hanlon, D.D.; "Rome and Pompeii," by Rev. J. G. Oakley, Ph.D.; "Pluck," by Rev. G. W. Miller, D.D.; "Blaise Pascal," by Rev. Wm. Jackson; "Language as related to the Mental Growth of the Child," by Prof. J. H. Hoose; "Teaching by Signs," by Rev. Lewellyn Pratt, D.D.; "Evolution of Living Being," by Prof. Wm. N. Rice.

sing with that remarkable grace and power for which he is so widely known.

In the history of the improvements at Round Lake those of the present year are more noticeable, availably useful, and significant of permanence than any previously made. The buildings which a number of large-hearted men and women have unostentatiously founded in the interests of religion and learning are particularly noteworthy.

Griffin Institute.

Griffin Institute, on the east side of Simpson Avenue, northwest of Hotel Wentworth, is in one of the most pleasant and secluded parts of the wide wood. In an environment of tall, fragrant-leafed trees, the handsome building discloses the varied features of its attractive architecture. The red color of the Philadelphia pressed brick of the first story and of the incasing slate of the second is in fine contrast with the foliage of the evergreens and the verdure of the north lawn. With a frontage of eighty-six feet and a depth of more than fifty, the building is not only outwardly imposing, but admirably fitted within for the uses of a summer school, for which it was erected. The eleven class-rooms on the first and second floors conveniently open by folding-doors into the spacious lecture-room, which is amply windowed with sky and side lights, and is well ventilated. Built in the fall of 1886 and completed in the summer of 1887, at an expense of more than $15,000, the institute is a substantial attestation of the personal interest taken in the higher education of young men and women by the honored giver, the Rev. William Griffin, D D., of West Troy, N. Y., the present president of the Round Lake Association.

George West Museum of Art and Archæology.

The most conspicuous of all the buildings on the grounds of the association is the George West Museum of Art and Archæology. It is also the most prominent artificial feature in the wide prospect of the wooded hills and cultivated uplands bordering the beautiful lake, of which from the high porticoes of the commanding structure there is a charming view. It was given the association by its philanthropic treasurer, the Hon. George West, of Ballston Spa. In its erection, in the spring of 1887, he generously expended $17,000. The lower hall, containing statuary, antiquities, curiosities, mineral and other cabinets, is ninety feet long, and forty-five wide. The

GEORGE WEST MUSEUM OF ART AND ARCHÆOLOGY.

gallery of paintings is of the same dimensions. The spacious rooms are admirably fitted for the exhibition of works of art and archæological treasures. At the north end of the building, adjoining the gallery of paintings, is a small studio for the use of artists and their pupils. The Grant memorials, loaned the association by Mrs. John P. Newman, are contained in an elaborate gilt cabinet, which she formally unveiled on Tuesday afternoon, July 12th, 1887. They include an excellent portrait of General Grant by Theodore Pine, of New York, and a fine engraving of the Nation's hero by William Edgar Marshall. The statuary comprises plaster casts of such masterpieces as the "Venus de Milo," "Venus de Medici," "Apollo Belvidere," "Fighting Gladiator," "Psyche," "Hebe," "Niobe," "Jupiter," "Mercury," "Diana," "Ajax," and "Laocoon." The loan collection of paintings embraces about one hundred in number, ranging in value severally from $100 to $2,500.[1]

The exhibition of Phœnician and Græco-Phœnician pottery exhumed at Cyprus by General L. P. di Cesnola, and the Assyro-Babylonian seal cylinders, ancient coin, intaglios, cameos, and other antiques, claim special attention.

The large collection of pictures illustrative of historic art, loaned by J. Leonard Corning, D.D., of Terre Haute, Ind., is exceedingly interesting and instructive. The display of more than three thousand differently-shaped pieces of wood, representing not less than one thousand kinds, is the valuable collection of the Rev. Charles Devol, M.D., of Albany. The attractive cabinet of Indian relics, which were collected by the late Hotia W. Farrar, of Swanton, Vt., the brother of the Rev. H. C. Farrar, D.D., is a rare archæological contribution.

In the mineral cabinets visitors will find many geological curiosities to interest them. The fac-similes of the great diamonds, representing their size and shape, are those of the Regent or Pitt, belonging to France, which weighs 136¼ carats and is valued at $625,000; the

---

[1] They were painted by the following well-known artists: William Sartain, Albert Bierstadt, A. F. Tait, Joseph Lyman, Burr H. Nicholls, Harry Eaton. G. H. McCord, Annie L. Morgan, George Inness, J. H. Dolph, R. W. Van Boskerck, A. S. Dillenbaugh, J. B. Bristol, A. Lownes, E. M. Scott, Maria Brooks, Gilbert Gaul, Benjamin R. Fitz, W. Deforest Bolmer, Rhoda Holmes Nicholls. Arthur Furlong, P. P. Ryder, William J. Whittemore. W. S. Macy, Mabel Olmsted, Warren Sheppard, Henry A. Ferguson, E. K. Baker, A. Beecher, Jno. A. McDougall, J. F. Cropsey, A. L. Crook, Ernest C. Rost, Francis C. Jones, C. E. Proctor, J. Wells Champney, M. A. Ackerman, W. S. Tyler, Mrs. S. J. C. Hitt, and Miss J. E. Cady.

Kohinoor (recut), England, 125 carats, $1,000,000; the Florentine, Austria, 139½ carats, $525,000; and the Orloff, Russia, 194¾ carats, $360,000. There is also a fac-simile of the largest nugget of gold ever found, which weighed 2,160 ounces and contained $41,883 worth of the precious metal. Among the other curiosities are casts of the Moabite stone, the black obelisk or Schalmaneser, the Siloam tablet, the Deluge tablet, the Rosetta stone, and a great winged lion of Nineveh.

On the east side of the south lawn and fronting on Peck Avenue is Garnsey Hall. The attractive three-story building, sixty-five feet wide and forty deep, was erected in the early summer of 1887 to afford the young women attending the Round Lake summer schools pleasant and inexpensive rooms. In it are thirty-two neatly-furnished bedrooms and two pretty parlors. Constructed at an outlay of more than $8,000, the hall obtains its name from Mrs. Caroline Garnsey, of West Troy, N. Y., by whose bounty it was built.

Kennedy Hall, recently built on the northwest corner of Whitfield Avenue and Ninth Street, modestly presents its graceful architecture to view on the south border of the stately grove. It inexpensively provides twenty-seven furnished dormitories and a convenient parlor for the accommodation of young men receiving instruction in the Round Lake Summer School. It is three stories high, forty feet wide and sixty-five deep. It was generously erected by Mrs. Nancy M. Kennedy, of Jonesville, N. Y., at a cost of $7,500.

ROUND LAKE ASSOCIATION.

The change of the name of the corporation from that of the Round Lake Camp-Meeting Association to that of the Round Lake Association was first contemplated in 1884. On November 5th, that year, the Rev. William Griffin, D.D., the Rev. Joseph E. King, D.D., and Charles D. Hammond were appointed a committee to apply to the Legislature of the State of New York for the passage of an act authorizing it. When, later, it was learned that the privilege could be granted by the County Court of Saratoga County, application was made to it. On July 8th, 1887, the Hon. J. S. L'Amoreaux issued the order to permit the corporation to take the name of the Round Lake Association, which order having been published, it was recorded July 19th, 1887.

The president of the association, the Rev. William Griffin, D.D.,

GARNSEY HALL.

in his address at the annual meeting on Wednesday, May 12th, 1887, felicitously remarked the changes in the affairs of the association :

"The Round Lake Camp-Meeting Association was born of a desire to find out and consecrate away from the busy haunts of men some local habitation for the pure worship of God and earnest Christian endeavor ; and it is believed that few places have been more signally owned and honored of God, than has this place during the brief period of its consecration as 'the mountain of the Lord's house.'
*   *   *   *

"Let no one, therefore, take alarm because we have dropped from our title the words 'Camp-Meeting,' as though we were about to change our character or abandon our distinctive works. We shorten our name because we have broadened our work. We are no longer a camp-meeting association merely, we are that in all that was intended by it in the beginning, but we are also more.

"Round Lake Association simple and comprehensive means the temple, beautiful for situation, the joy of all beholders in the place

KENNEDY HALL.

of the Tabernacle and tents in the wilderness. Another advance step is that modification of our organic law by which we invite to the fellowship of our counsels, in our board of trustees, persons not members of the Methodist Church. Henceforth this place will be known, not as a 'Methodist Camp Ground,' but a 'Christian Summer Home,' where there is neither Methodist nor Presbyterian, Baptist nor Congregationalist, Episcopalian nor Dutch Reformed, but where the brotherhood of Christ shall dwell together in unity, provoking one another only by 'love and good works.'   *   *   *   *

"Our Sunday-School Assembly, to be known hereafter in the series of summer sessions as 'Round Lake Assembly,' needs no introduction at this time. It has attained its majority, and made a reputation for itself second to none in the land, in the scope and excellence of its work.   *   *   *   *

"Our Summer School, which came to many of us last year so unexpectedly and behaved itself so well that it completely won our confidence and challenged our admiration, and led us to exclaim, 'it is good for us that it should be here, let us build for it tabernacles,' has, I am happy to say, consented to stay. The wonderful success of the first term was a surprise and joy to everybody."

Summer Homes.

The advantages of Round Lake as a place of summer residence are superior in many ways to those of other rural seats. They may be concisely presented in a brief summary. First, as respects the grounds: They are frequently, conveniently, and inexpensively accessible by railroad. In part, they are shaded, mostly by high-foliaged trees, under which cool, refreshing breezes waft the salubrious fragrance of the pines and other evergreens. They are evenly graded, and no depressions harbor stagnant water. The soil is gravelly, and the paths and avenues are never muddy after rainfalls. A well-devised system of sewers effects the removal of refuse, liquids, and deleterious matter. In every part of the sunny-aisled wood cultivated flowers bloom with color as brilliant as those growing in unshaded places.

The tameness of the unmolested squirrels, which partake of food from the open hands of friendly givers, and the undisturbed presence of many warbling birds, always delight sojourners and visitors.

The wide expanse of the lake affords all the pleasures of yachting and rowing. Bass and other fish in its waters invite angling.

HON. GALEN R. HITT'S COTTAGE.

Drives to Saratoga Lake, five miles away, and along shady, brook-margined country roads, are also enjoyable.

The mineral water of Round Lake has the same properties as that of the famous Congress fountain of Saratoga Springs. The limpid water of the constantly-flowing springs in the southwestern part of the grounds, supplied the cottages and drinking fountains, is as much appreciated for its refreshing coolness as it is for its exceeding purity and wholesomeness.

The expense of acquiring property at Round Lake is a matter of special consideration. The price of eligible building lots within or without the grove is low, and the cost of the erection of a cottage is limited by the purpose of the builder. Persons seeking the enjoyment of shade and seclusion can purchase sites in different parts of the spacious wood; those desiring far-reaching prospects, a view of the placid lake, and a wide survey of the cloud-featured sky, can buy lots in the open and elevated parts of the extensive grounds. Those who may wish to spend a summer or a vacation at Round Lake can, by timely application, obtain the use of a cottage at a nominal rent, or secure first-class accommodations at Hotel Wentworth, or cozy rooms at the different boarding-houses at moderate rates.

At Round Lake there are no imperative dictations of fashion. A woman's plain toilet does not subject her to disagreeable criticism, and children may enjoy the freedom of the healthful retreat in simple, home-worn clothing. The infrequency of horses and vehicles, and the absence of cats and dogs on the grounds, greatly lessen the watchful care of small children at play out-doors.

ROUND LAKE.

BY REV. BISHOP EDMUND S. JANES, NEW YORK, 1875.

O God! our temple thou hast made,
 Its floor of earth by Thee was laid;
Its leafy roof and pillars grand
 Are all the work of Thy own hand.

Its ornaments of hill and lake
 Are such as none but Thou couldst make;
Its living fountain, bright and free,
 Could only have its source in Thee.

The beauties of our sacred shrine
 Declare its Architect divine;
And when Thy presence, Lord, is given,
 It is to us the gate of Heav'n.

Then let Thy saving pow'r be known,
 And here Thy richest grace be shown;
May thousands here be born to God
 And thousands washed in Jesus' blood.

ROUND LAKE.

BY JOHN C. BLAIR.

(1878.)

I love its grand majestic wood,
 Its dusky twilight dimness;
The reverential thought it brings,
 Its awe-inspiring stillness;
Dear to my heart its swaying trees,
 Whose music low and tender
Is wafted up to God above,
 Free from cathedral splendor.

No temple reared by human hands,
 The wealth of art revealing,
Could e'er produce such holy thought,
 Such calm and peaceful feeling;
No costly organ peal elate,
 Or set the pulses bounding,
Like olden anthem, sweet and clear,
 Through leafy aisles resounding.

The silvery moon with radiant light
 Her nightly vigils keeping,
Reveals her lovely counterpart
 In mirrored beauty sleeping;

And lingers like a maiden coy
  O'er meadow brook-side kneeling,
Who finds the water 'neath her gaze
  Her own sweet self revealing.

The golden glory of the sun,
  The western sky adorning,
The east aglow with rosy light,
  The herald of the morning;
The twilight hour of pensive thought,
  The soul from sin alluring,
All tend to make this lovely spot
  An Eden most enduring.

From Memory's page we oft recall
  The dear old-fashioned meetings,
'While tenting on the old camp ground,'
  Rich with its cordial greetings,
The melody of singing birds
  With sacred music blending,
The solemn voice beneath the trees
  In holy prayer ascending.

We love its quiet forest lake,
  A gem in emerald setting,
Its crystal surface calm and still,
  The heavens above reflecting,
As if from out yon starry dome
  A jewel bright in falling
Had lent new beauty to the scene,
  An added charm installing.

HYMNS.

Composed for and sung during the first Fraternal Meeting, July, 1874.

THE DAY OF DAYS.

BY REV. F. BOTTOME, D.D.

1. Praise ye the Lord! O sing aloud!
    The strong Redeemer's name declare,
  And thankful lift your incense-cloud
    In blended gift of praise and prayer.

2. His own right arm hath safely led
    Our scatter'd tribes through all the way;
  And lo, with joyful feet we tread
    The courts His hands have raised, to-day.

3. One God, one faith, one name we own,
    One family in Him we meet;
  His love and fellowship make known
    In sweet communion at His feet.

4. Our fathers' God! with one desire,
    Our hands upraised to Thee behold!
   We wait the pentecostal fire
    That marked our sires in days of old.

5. So shall this forest-temple ring,
    And yon blue dome resound Thy praise;
   And this, while Thy great name we sing,
    Shall be to us the day of days.

CHRISTIAN GREETING.

BY MRS. JOSEPH HILLMAN.

1. From many a Christian nation,
    And many a distant clime;
   From India's sunny region,
    They come with love divine.
   From snow-clad Rocky Mountains,
    And islands of the sea,
   From Ganges' sacred river,
    To worship only Thee.

2. The wondrous star of Bethlehem
    Shines with a lustre clear,
   The dew of Hermon resting
    Like holy incense here.
   Jesus! the place is sacred!
    We here tread holy ground;
   Lift high the blood-stained banner,
    With glorious victory crowned!

3. Come, then—we bid you welcome—
    Ye sacramental host;
   Salvation is our watchword,
    In God we put our trust.
   As North and South together,
    With East and West we meet,
   The star of hope shines brightly,
    Fraternally we greet.

4. We bathe in Judah's fountain—
    A balm for all our woes;
   The blood of Christ it cleanseth—
    For all the world it flows.
   The spicy gales of Calvary
    Bring healing by the way;
   "Salvation! O salvation!"
    Proclaim the joyful day.

DEVOTION.

BY E. A. PECK.

1. O Thou, the everliving God,
    Help us Thy praise to sing;
    Then shall these consecrated groves
    With hallelujahs ring.

Cho.: O praise the Lord, with one accord,
    Exhalt His name, His love proclaim;
    His promise sure, and will endure,
    Forever more—forever more.

2. We thank Thee for this glorious day,
    From North and South we come;
    From East and West we hear the cry.
    God's people shall be one.

3. Baptize us with Thy Spirit, Lord;
    O send the sacred fire.
    Then shall we speak with other tongues
    If only God inspire.

CHRISTIAN UNITY.

BY REV. A. C. ROSE.

1. God of our fathers, from Thy throne,
    Look down and bless us while we pray!
    We join in praising Thee as one,
    Within this hallowed grove to-day.

2. Are we not all the sons of God?
    And heirs alike of heavenly love?
    Washed by the same all-cleansing blood,
    And traveling to *one* home above?

3. Baptize us, then, into one mind—
    The mind, O Christ, which is in Thee:
    And into sweetest union bind
    Our hearts, in love and sympathy.

4. Thus while we wait together here,
    Beneath this sacred leafy shade,
    We all shall feel Thy presence near
    And see Thy saving power displayed.

5. Grant this, and when we hence remove,
    Our hearts shall still united be
    Till we shall meet again above,
    And endless praises give to Thee.

OPENING DAY AT ROUND LAKE.

(July 12th, 1887.)

By Joseph E. King, D.D.

To him his meed of glory and of bliss—
'Twas Joseph Hillman who began all this.
The Projector he, Columbus of Round Lake,
His just renown let none presume to take.
The Nations came to worship in our grove,
And North and South joined in fraternal love.
What giants thundered and what seraphs blazed,
Heaven oft rejoiced while hell stood back amazed!
In aftertime, when storm-clouds reared their crest,
A bow of promise shone from out the West.
While many hands brought each their willing gift,
To lay the spectre, and our debt to lift,
One princely hand paid more than all the rest,
Thus came deliverance from the bounteous West.
And now, to crown this largeness of the heart,
Behold arise yon Museum of Art!
Fair and complete and worthy of the giver,
A thing of beauty and a joy forever.
Than William Griffin lives no worthier name
To grace the bulwarks of our rising fame,
A sacred tryst for better or for worse
Commands his prayers, his counsels and his purse,
To endow the Assembly and our Summer Schools,
Fair structures rise—his ardor never cools.
While others dreamed, his bent it was to act,
He waved his wand, and lo, the accomplished fact!
Last year a promise, but to-day the fruit,
We hail with joy the "Griffin" Institute.
And not content, to further noble ends
He gives himself and implicates his friends.
Two stately halls, the Institute's annex,
Fair contributions from the gentler sex,
"Garnsey" and "Kennedy," inscribe on either portal,
Thus link to youth and surely make immortal.
Long may these walls wisdom enforce and truth
To widening circles of our goodly youth;
While lake and wood, and towers and bending skies
Make this fair spot the scholar's Paradise!

OFFICERS
OF
THE ROUND LAKE CAMP-MEETING ASSOCIATION.

Presidents.

Joseph Hillman... ....from May 1, 1868, to April 27, 1881.
Rev. Rodman H. Robinson, D.D........from April 27, 1881, to October 19, 1886.
Rev. William Griffin, D.D.............from November 3, 1886, to July 19, 1887.

Vice-Presidents.

Charles W. Pierce......................from May 4, 1868, to March 30, 1870.
Prof. H. A. Wilson.....................from March 30, 1870, to May 5, 1886.

First Vice-President.

Prof. H. A. Wilson.................. ....from May 5, 1886, to July 19, 1887.

Second Vice-Presidents.

Rev. William Griffin, D.D......... ...from July 24, 1885, to November 3, 1886.
Charles D. Hammond...............from November 3, 1886, to July 19, 1887.

Secretaries.

E. O. Howland..........................from May 4, 1868, to March 29, 1871.
Phineas S Pettit .. .. .from March 29, 1871, to March 25, 1874.
Warren S. Kelley.... ....from March 25, 1874, to May 9, 1881.
Rev. B. B. Loomis.... ....from May 9, 1881, to May 3, 1882.
Warren S. Kelley............. ....from May 3, 1882, to July 19, 1887.

Treasurers.

George Bristol........................from May 4, 1868, to   , 1868.
E. A. Hartshorn....... ....from December 16, 1868, to February 26, 1878.
George W. Horton..................from February 26, 1878, to April 30, 1879.
Rev. Samuel McKean, D.D.............from April 30, 1879, to April 27, 1881.
Hon. George West.....................from April 27, 1881, to July 19, 1887.

Trustees.
1868-9.

First Class: Hazen W. Bennett, George Bristol, James H. Earl, E. O. Howland, Robert N. Newton, Ephraim D. Waldron, Levi Weed, M.D., elected May 4th, 1868.

Rev. Jesse T. Peck, D.D., elected to fill place of James H. Earl. December 16th, 1868.

Second Class: George L. Clark, Robert Coburn, Roscius R. Kennedy, Samuel Martin, William H. McEchron, Phineas S. Pettit, Jesse Wilson, elected May 4th, 1868.

Third Class: William Dalton, Joseph Hillman, F. D. Hodgeman, Gardner Howland, Rev. Joseph E. King, D.D., Charles W. Pierce, H. A. Wilson, elected May 4th, 1868.

Rev. William Griffin, D.D., elected to fill place of William Dalton, December 16th, 1868.

1869-70.

First Class: Hazen W. Bennett, E. A. Hartshorn, E. O. Howland, Robert N. Newton, Rev. Jesse T. Peck, D.D., Ephraim D. Waldron, George West, elected March 31st, 1869.

Second Class: George L. Clark, Robert Coburn, Roscius R. Kennedy, Samuel Martin, William H. McEchron, Phineas S. Pettit, Jesse Wilson, elected May 4th, 1868.

Third Class: Joseph Hillman, F. D. Hodgeman, Gardner Howland, Rev. Joseph E. King, D.D., Charles W. Pierce, H. A. Wilson, elected May 4th, 1868. Rev. William Griffin, D.D., elected December 16th, 1868.

1870-1.

First Class: Hazen W. Bennett, E. A. Hartshorn, E. O. Howland, Robert N. Newton, Rev. Jesse T. Peck, D.D., Ephraim D. Waldron, George West, elected March 31st, 1869.

Second Class: Robert Coburn, Samuel E. Howe, Samuel Martin, William H. McEchron, Phineas S. Pettit, Rev. Ensign Stover, Jesse Wilson, elected June 21st, 1870.

Third Class: Joseph Hillman, T. D. Hodgeman, Gardner Howland, Rev. Joseph E. King, D.D., Charles W. Pierce, H. A. Wilson, elected May 4th, 1868; Rev. William Griffin, D.D., elected December 16th, 1868.

1871-2.

First Class: Hazen W. Bennett, E. A. Hartshorn, E. O. Howland, Robert N. Newton, Rev. Jesse T. Peck, D.D., Ephraim D. Waldron, George West, elected March 31st, 1869.

Second Class: Robert Coburn, Samuel E. Howe, Samuel Martin, William H. McEchron, Phineas S. Pettit, Rev. Ensign Stover, Jesse Wilson, elected June 21st, 1870.

John W. Osborn elected to fill place of Rev. Ensign Stover, July 5th, 1871.

Third Class: Rev. William Griffin, D.D., Joseph Hillman, F. D. Hodgeman, Gardner Howland, Rev. Joseph E. King, D.D., Jacob Travis, H. A. Wilson, elected March 29th, 1871.

1872-3.

First Class: Hazen W. Bennett, S. M. Birch, E. A. Hartshorn, E. O. Howland, Robert N. Newton, William Shepherd, Ephraim D. Waldron, elected April 10th, 1872.

Charles H. Smith, M.D., elected to fill place of S. M. Birch, July, 17th, 1872.

Second Class: Robert Coburn, Samuel E. Howe, Samuel Martin, William H. McEchron, Phineas S. Pettit, Jesse Wilson, elected June 21st, 1870; John W. Osborn, July 5th, 1871.

Third Class: Rev. William Griffin, D.D., Joseph Hillman, F. D. Hodgeman, Gardner Howland, Rev. Joseph E. King, D.D., Jacob Travis, H. A. Wilson, elected March 29th, 1871.

1873-4.

First Class: Hazen W. Bennett, E. A. Hartshorn, E. O. Howland, Robert N. Newton, William Shepherd, Ephraim D. Waldron, elected April 10th, 1872.
George West elected to fill place of C. H. Smith, M.D., March 26th, 1873.
Second Class: Warren S. Kelley, Samuel Martin, Phineas S. Pettit, John W. Osborn, William Renne, E. Robinson, Jesse Wilson, elected March 26th, 1873.
Third Class: Rev. William Griffin, D.D., Joseph Hillman, F. D. Hodgeman, Gardner Howland, Rev. Joseph E. King, D.D., Jacob Travis, H. A. Wilson, elected March 29th, 1871.

1874-5.

First Class: Hazen W. Bennett, E. A. Hartshorn, E. O. Howland, Robert N. Newton, William Shepherd, Ephraim D. Waldron, elected April 10th, 1872; George West, March 26th, 1873.
Rev. Joseph E. King elected in place of William Shepherd, June 3d, 1874.
Second Class: Warren S. Kelley, Samuel Martin, Phineas S. Pettit, John W. Osborn, Jesse Wilson, elected March 26th, 1873; George W. Hoxsie elected in place of E. Robinson, March 25th, 1874.
John D. Rogers elected in place of William Renne, March 25th, 1874; Rev. Bernice D. Ames elected in place of John D. Rogers, June 3d, 1874.
Third Class: Rev. Bernice D. Ames, George B. Cluett, Rev. William Griffin, D.D., Joseph Hillman, Rev. Joseph E. King, Jacob Travis, H. A. Wilson, elected March 25th, 1874.
William Shepherd, elected in place of Rev. Bernice D. Ames, June 3d, 1874; John D. Rogers, elected in place of Rev. Joseph E. King, D.D., June 3d, 1874.

1875-6.

First Class: Hazen W. Bennett, Thomas Farwell, E. A. Hartshorn, Daniel Hays, Rev. Joseph E. King, D.D., Robert N. Newton, George West, elected April 28th, 1875.
Second Class: Warren S. Kelley, Samuel Martin, Phineas S. Pettit, John W. Osborn, Jesse Wilson, elected March 26th, 1873; George W. Hoxsie, March 25th, 1874; Rev. Bernice D. Ames, June 3d, 1874.
Third Class: George B. Cluett, Rev. William Griffin, D.D., Joseph Hillman, Jacob Travis, H. A. Wilson, elected March 25th, 1874; John D. Rogers and William Shepherd, elected June 3d, 1874.

1876-7.

First Class: Hazen W. Bennett, Thomas Farwell, E. A. Hartshorn, Daniel Hays, Rev. Joseph E. King, D.D., Robert N. Newton, George West, elected April 28th, 1875.
Second Class: George W. Horton, Warren S. Kelley, Abram Le Gallez, John W. Osborn, Phineas S. Pettit, Rev. Sanford Washburn, Jesse Wilson, elected April 26th, 1876.
Third Class: George B. Cluett, Rev. William Griffin, D.D., Joseph Hillman, Jacob Travis, H. A. Wilson, elected March 25th, 1874; John D. Rogers and William Shepherd elected June 3d, 1874.
Edmund Cluett elected in place of George B. Cluett, June 28th, 1876.

1877-8.

First Class: Hazen W. Bennett, Thomas Farwell, E. A. Hartshorn, Daniel Hays, Rev. Joseph E. King, D.D., Robert N. Newton, George West, elected April 28th, 1875.

Daniel Klock, jr., elected in place of Daniel Hays; George G. Saxe in place of E. A. Hartshorn, and Harvey Wendell in place of Hazen W. Bennett, February 26th, 1878.

Second Class: George W. Horton, Warren S. Kelley, Abram Le Gallez, John W. Osborn, Phineas S. Pettit, Rev. Sanford Washburn, Jesse Wilson, elected April 26th, 1876.

Rev. R. H. Robinson elected in place of Rev. Sanford Washburn, February 26th, 1878.

Third Class: Oliver Boutwell, Edmund Cluett, Rev. William Griffin, D.D., Joseph Hillman, John D. Rogers, Jacob Travis, H. A. Wilson, elected April 25th, 1877.

Perrin W. Converse elected in place of Edmund Cluett, and Silas Owen in place of Jacob Travis, February 26th, 1878.

1878-9.

First Class: Thomas Farwell, Rev. Joseph E. King, D.D., Daniel Klock, jr., Robert N. Newton, George G. Saxe, Harvey Wendell, George West, elected April 24th, 1878.

Second Class: George W. Horton, Warren S. Kelley, Abram Le Gallez, John W. Osborn, Phineas S. Pettit, Jesse Wilson, elected April 26th, 1876; Rev. R. H. Robinson elected February 26th, 1878.

Samuel F. Harris elected in place of Jesse Wilson April 24th, 1878.

Third Class: Oliver Boutwell, Rev. William Griffin, D.D., Joseph Hillman, John D. Rogers, H. A. Wilson, elected April 25th, 1877; Perrin W. Converse and Silas Owen elected February 26th, 1878.

N. S. Vedder elected in place of Rev. William Griffin, D.D., September 5th, 1878.

1879-80.

First Class: Thomas Farwell, Rev. Joseph E. King, D.D., Daniel Klock, jr., Robert N. Newton, George G. Saxe, Harvey Wendell, George West, elected April 24th, 1878.

Second Class: Abram Le Gallez, Samuel F. Harris, George W. Horton, Warren S. Kelley, Henry Kelly, Phineas S. Pettit, Rev. R. H. Robinson, elected April 30th, 1879.

Third Class: Oliver Boutwell, Joseph Hillman, John D. Rogers, H. A. Wilson, elected April 25th, 1877; Perrin W. Converse and Silas Owen elected February 26th, 1878; N. S. Vedder elected September 5th, 1878.

1880-1.

First Class: Thomas Farwell, Rev. Joseph E. King, D.D., Daniel Klock, jr., Robert N. Newton, George G. Saxe, Harvey Wendell, George West, elected April 24th, 1878.

Rev. H. C. Farrar elected in place of George G. Saxe, and Charles D. Hammond in place of Daniel Klock, jr., March 8th, 1881.

Second Class: Abram Le Gallez, Samuel F. Harris, George W. Horton, Warren S. Kelley, Henry Kelly, Phineas S. Pettit, Rev. R. H. Robinson, elected April 30th, 1879.

Third Class: Oliver Boutwell, Perrin W. Converse, Rev. Joel W. Eaton, Joseph Hillman, Silas Owen, John D. Rogers, H. A. Wilson, elected April 28th, 1880.

Rev. William Griffin, D.D., elected in place of Joel W. Eaton, March 8th, 1881.

1881-2.

First Class: Edmund Cluett, James W. Eaton, Edmund C. Edmonds, Rev. H. C. Farrar, Charles D. Hammond, Rev. Joseph E. King, D.D., George West, elected April 27th, 1881.

Second Class: Abram Le Gallez, Samuel F. Harris, George W. Horton, Warren S. Kelley, Henry Kelly, Phineas S. Pettit, Rev. R. H. Robinson, elected April 30th, 1879.

Third Class: Oliver Boutwell, Perrin W. Converse, Joseph Hillman, Silas Owen, John D. Rogers, H. A. Wilson, elected April 28th, 1880; Rev. William Griffin, D.D., elected March 8th, 1881.

1882-3.

First Class: Edmund Cluett, James W. Eaton, Edmund C. Edmonds, Rev. H. C. Farrar, Charles D. Hammond, Rev. Joseph E. King, D.D., George West, elected April 27th, 1881.

Second Class: Rev. Cabot M. Clark, Benjamin Cooper, Charles Cooper, Abram Le Gallez, Warren S. Kelley, Henry Kelly, R. H. Robinson, elected May 3d, 1882.

Third Class: Oliver Boutwell, Perrin W. Converse, Joseph Hillman, Silas Owen, John D. Rogers, H. A. Wilson, elected April 28th, 1880; Rev. William Griffin, D.D., elected March 8th, 1881.

1883-4.

First Class: Edmund Cluett, James W. Eaton, Edmund C. Edmonds, Rev. H. C. Farrar, Charles D. Hammond, Rev. Joseph E. King, D.D., George West, elected April 27th, 1881.

Second Class: Rev. Cabot M. Clark, Benjamin Cooper, Charles Cooper, Abram Le Gallez, Warren S. Kelley, Henry Kelly, R. H. Robinson, elected May 3d, 1882.

Third Class: Oliver Boutwell, Perrin W. Converse, Rev. William Griffin, D.D., Joseph Hillman, Silas Owen, John D. Rogers, H. A. Wilson, elected May 2d, 1883.

1884-5.

First Class: Edmund C. Edmonds, Rev. H. C. Farrar, Charles D. Hammond, Rev. Joseph E. King, D.D., Robert N. Newton, Rev. R. H. Robinson, George West, elected May 7th, 1884.

Second Class: Rev. Cabot M. Clark, Benjamin Cooper, Charles Cooper, Abram Le Gallez, Warren S. Kelley, Henry Kelly, R. H. Robinson, elected May 3d, 1882. Rev. S. V. Leech, D.D., elected in place of Abram Le Gallez, and E. A. Hartshorn in place of Rev. R. H. Robinson, May 7th, 1884.

Third Class: Oliver Boutwell, Perrin W. Converse, Rev. William Griffin, D.D., Joseph Hillman, Silas Owen, John D. Rogers, H. A. Wilson, elected May 2d, 1883.

1885-6.

First Class : Edmund C. Edmonds, Rev. H. C. Farrar, Charles D. Hammond, Rev. Joseph E. King, D.D., Robert N. Newton, Rev. R. H. Robinson, George West, elected May 7th, 1884.

Second Class : Rev. Cabot M. Clark, J. W. A. Cluett, Benjamin Cooper, Charles Cooper, E. A. Hartshorn, Warren S. Kelley, Rev. Andrew McGilton, elected May 6th, 1885.

Third Class : Oliver Boutwell, Perrin W. Converse, Rev. William Griffin, D.D., Joseph Hillman, Silas Owen, John D. Rogers, H. A. Wilson, elected May 2d, 1883.

1886-7.

First Class : Edmund C. Edmonds, Rev. H. C. Farrar, D.D., Charles D. Hammond, Rev. Joseph E. King, D.D., Robert A. Newton, Rev. R. H. Robinson, George West, elected May 7th, 1884.

Rev. John P. Newman, D.D., elected in place of Rev. R. H. Robinson, D.D., November 3d, 1886.

Second Class : Rev. Cabot M. Clark, J. W. A. Cluett, Benjamin Cooper, Charles Cooper, E. A. Hartshorn, Warren S. Kelley, Rev. Andrew McGilton, elected May 6th, 1885.

Third Class : Oliver Boutwell, Perrin W. Converse, Rev. William Griffin, D.D., Joseph Hillman, Silas Owen, John D. Rogers, H. A. Wilson, elected May 5th, 1886.

1887—to July 19th.

First Class : Rev. H. C. Farrar, D.D., Charles D. Hammond, Rev. Joseph E. King, D.D., Rev. John P. Newman, D.D., Robert N. Newton, M. B. Sherman, George West, elected May 11th, 1887.

Second Class : Rev. Cabot M. Clark, J. W. A. Cluett, Benjamin Cooper, Charles Cooper, E. A. Hartshorn, Warren S. Kelley, Rev. Andrew McGilton, elected May 6th, 1885.

Third Class : Oliver Boutwell, Perrin W. Converse, Rev. William Griffin, D.D., Joseph Hillman, Silas Owen, John D. Rogers, H. A. Wilson, elected May 5th, 1886.

Superintendents.

Lewis Gage..from 1868 to April 1, 1874.
John D. Rogers...........................from April 1, 1874 to July 19, 1887.

OFFICERS
OF
THE ROUND LAKE ASSOCIATION,
From July 19th, 1887, to present time.

Rev. William Griffin, D.D., West Troy, N. Y........................*President.*
Prof. H. A Wilson, Saratoga Springs, N. Y..............*First Vice-President.*
Charles D. Hammond, Albany, N. Y....................*Second Vice-President.*
Warren S. Kelley, Albany, N. Y..*Secretary.*
Hon. George West, Ballston Spa....................................*Treasurer.*

TRUSTEES.
First Class.
Rev. H. C. Farrar, D.D..West Troy, N. Y.
Charles D. Hammond...Albany, N. Y.
Rev. Joseph E. King, D.D..Fort Edward, N. Y.
Rev. John P. Newman, D.D......................................Washington, D. C.
Robert N. Newton..Albany, N. Y.
M. B. Sherman...Albany, N. Y.
Hon. George West..Ballston Spa, N. Y.

Second Class.
Rev. Cabot M. Clark..Clifton Park, N. Y.
J. W. A. Cluett..Troy, N. Y.
Benjamin Cooper..Troy, N. Y.
Charles Cooper..Bennington, Vt.
E. A. Hartshorn..Troy, N. Y.
Warren S. Kelley...Albany, N. Y.
Rev. Andrew McGilton...West Troy, N. Y.

Third Class.
Oliver Boutwell..Troy, N. Y.
Perrin W. Converse...Troy, N. Y.
Rev. William Griffin, D.D.......................................West Troy, N. Y.
Joseph Hillman..Troy, N. Y.
Silas Owen..Cohoes, N. Y.
John D. Rogers..Round Lake, N. Y.
H. A. Wilson...Saratoga Springs, N. Y.

TRUSTEES, *ex-officio*[1].
Rev. J. W. Bennett..Brandon, Vt.
Rev. Joel W. Eaton, D.D...Glens' Falls, N. Y.
Rev. D. W. Gates..Albany, N. Y.
Rev. A. D. Heaxt...Plattsburgh, N. Y.
Rev. Samuel McKean, D.D....................................Lansingburgh, N. Y.
Rev. Samuel Meredith..Green Island, N. Y.

Superintendent.
John D. Rogers...Round Lake, N. Y.

[1] The presiding elders of the Troy Conference are *ex-officio* members of the board of trustees.

Young · Men · and · Young · Women

Who have attended the Summer School at Round Lake should finish at the

Troy Business College,

for here they can complete Stenography, Typewriting and Telegraphy, or take the most thorough Business Course. Graduates from this Institution have never before been in so great demand.

For catalogue containing full information, address

McCREARY & SHIELDS,
NO. 13 THIRD STREET,

TROY, N. Y.

Respecting the merits of our school we refer to Dr. J. H. Worman, Director of the Round Lake Summer School.

FORT ✢ EDWARD

Collegiate Institute

Rebuilt and refurnished in 1881, at a cost of $72,000, is now perhaps the handsomest and best appointed Boarding Seminary in the state. Average enrollments for past five years, 185 per term, of whom 100 have been boarding students.

Six Courses of Study are provided—College preparatory, Commercial, Scientific, Latin Scientific, Classical and Eclectic.

Graduates of High Schools and other advanced students are cordially welcomed to our Senior Classes, and find a year at our institute to be both greatly enjoyable and profitable.

The bible and evangelical religion are not apologized for, but endorsed and recommended. The three evening religious meetings of each week of the school year are designed to be revival meetings, and God greatly blesses these regular means of grace.

Four live Literary Societies—two of gentlemen and two of ladies—with o.r constant morning chapel readings and recitations and our frequent literary and oratorical contests serve powerfully to awaken and develop the speaking and writing fluently of our students.

Music, Painting and Modern Languages also receive conspicuous attention.

For charges and full information, see new catalogue. For special rates to preachers and to two or more students from same family, please correspond with the Principal,

JOS. E. KING, D. D.,

FORT EDWARD. N. Y.

THE
ACADEMY
OF
SARATOGA COUNTY.

MECHANICVILLE, N. Y.

Healthful Location,

Thorough Instruction,

Three Courses of Study,

College Preparatory,

Latin Scientific, Scientific.

For Circulars or Catalogues apply to

MRS. S. E. KING-AMES,
PRINCIPAL.

For Grandeur, Beauty and Healthfulness, no Region in the World
COMPARES WITH

Lake George and the Adirondack Mountains,

ELIZABETHTOWN, KEENE VALLEY, LAKE PLACID, LOON,
SARANAC, ST. REGIS, CHATEAUGAY LAKES, ETC.

THE ONLY DIRECT LINE TO THIS PARADISE OF THE HEALTH AND PLEASURE SEEKER IS VIA

The Delaware & Hudson R. R.

"THE FAVORITE TOURISTS' ROUTE"

To SARATOGA, ROUND LAKE,
LAKE CHAMPLAIN, AUSABLE CHASM,
SHARON SPRINGS, COOPERSTOWN,
AND THE CELEBRATED

GRAVITY RAILROAD

BETWEEN
CARBONDALE and HONESDALE, PA.

The Shortest and Most Comfortable Route between
New York & Montreal, and between Albany, Elmira, Corning and the Oil Regions.

Send 5-cent Stamp for Hotel and Boarding House List, Guide, Maps, etc.

H. G. YOUNG, Gen'l Manager.　　　J. W. BURDICK, Gen'l Passenger Agent.

ALBANY, N. Y.

SARATOGA,
Capt. ABRAMS.

CITY OF TROY,
Capt. WOLCOTT.

CITIZENS' LINE--TROY TO NEW YORK.

NEW STEAMERS.

CITIZENS EVENING LINE
ON THE HUDSON RIVER

DAILY FROM TROY (except Saturdays), on arrival of Delaware & Hudson evening train. **Sundays at 6 P. M.**
From **NEW YORK DAILY** (except Saturdays), at **6 P. M.**, from PIER 44, foot Christopher Street.

FARE ALWAYS LOWER THAN BY ANY OTHER ROUTE.

Elegant State Room, $1 AND $2.   Best and Cheapest Route to Ocean Grove and all Seaside Resorts.

GEO. W. GIBSON, Gen'l Pass'r Agent, Troy.   G. W. HORTON, Vice-President, Troy.

IRA H. CARPENTER.   C. H. BALL.

Troy Pottery & Sewer Pipe Co.

ESTABLISHED 1809.

CARPENTER & BALL,

(Successors to WALTER J. SEYMOUR),

Salt Glazed Vitrified Sewer

—AND—

DRAIN PIPE

102 FERRY STREET,

TROY, N. Y.

N. B.—The Company has supplied the Round Lake Association with Sewer Pipe.

J. M. WARREN & CO.
Hardware, Iron, Nails.

J M. W. Old Process Roofing Tin.

Builders' Hardware and Tools.

Lawn Mowers, Rakes and Settees.

Garden Hose and Reels.

Window and Door Screens.

TROY, N. Y.

ALSO PROPRIETORS OF

The Troy Stamping Works
HOUSE FURNISHING GOODS.

Our stock comprises the largest and most complete assortment (including all the latest novelties in house-keeping utensils) to be found anywhere, such as

Tin, Copper, Brass,
Enamelled, Wooden, Willow and other Wares,

OF OUR OWN AND OTHER MANUFACTURE.

Goods all first-class and at reasonable prices. An inspection of our stock is invited.

245 & 247 RIVER ST.,
TROY, N. Y.

The + Revivalist.

A CHOICE COLLECTION OF REVIVAL HYMNS AND TUNES, ORIGINAL AND SELECTED

—BY—

JOSEPH HILLMAN,

AUTHOR OF

"Sunday School Hymns and Revival Choruses."

CLOTH, 75c.

"This, we think, is one of the best selections of revival melodies we have met with."—*The Guide to Holiness.*
"It is among the very best of its kind."—*The Christian Advocate.*

SOLD BY

PHILLIPS & HUNT,
M. E. BOOK CONCERN,
805 BROADWAY, NEW YORK, N. Y.

HOW CAN I BE SAVED?

BY

JOSEPH HILLMAN,

CLOTH, 40c.

THIS LITTLE VOLUME IS DESIGNED FOR THOSE WHO DESIRE TO KNOW HOW THEY CAN BE SAVED, HOW THEY MAY BE ASSURED OF A PRESENT SALVATION, AND HOW THEY MAY BE KEPT THEREIN.

"It will be of great service to seekers for the truth and to those engaged in directing others in the search."—*Rev. E. Wentworth, D. D.*

SOLD BY

PHILLIPS & HUNT,
M. E. BOOK CONCERN,
805 BROADWAY, NEW YORK, N. Y.

John L. Thompson, Sons & Co.,

ESTABLISHED 1797.

WHOLESALE DEALERS

IN

PURE LINSEED OIL, PURE LEAD,

MIXED PAINTS, COLORS,

VARNISHES, GLASS,

PAINT

AND

Artists' Brushes.

ALSO

A FULL ASSORTMENT OF

PURE DRUGS AND MEDICINES.

159, 161, 163 RIVER STREET,
TROY, N. Y.

CLUETT'S

CROWN COLLARS,

CUFFS, and

MONARCH   MONARCH

SHIRTS,

ARE THE BEST OF ALL.

GEO. B. CLUETT, BRO. & CO.,
TROY, N. Y.

Wheeler & Wilson Mfg. Co's

SEWING AND BUTTON-HOLE

MACHINES.

The only full line of machines for all kinds of family sewing and all grades of manufacturing that will sew any stitchable material, from the finest gauze to the heaviest leather.

A specialty made of supplying Factories with Shafting, Power Transmitters, Pulleys, Belting, Oil, Needles, Sewing Machine parts and special attachments; in fact, we supply anything pertaining to a Sewing Machine. See our new family and manufacturing machines before you purchase. It will pay you.

If you want anything pertaining to a Machine call on us.

Wheeler & Wilson Mfg. Co.

SALESROOMS:

454 & 456 FULTON ST., TROY.

AGENTS WANTED WHERE NOT REPRESENTED.

Russell House,

Corner Wesley Ave. & Third St.

Round Lake, N. Y.

ESTABLISHED 1877.

BOARD AND ROOMS BY THE DAY OR WEEK
AT MODERATE PRICES.

Miss H. A. Russell.

W. A. SHERMAN,

TROY,

259 RIVER ST.

N. Y.

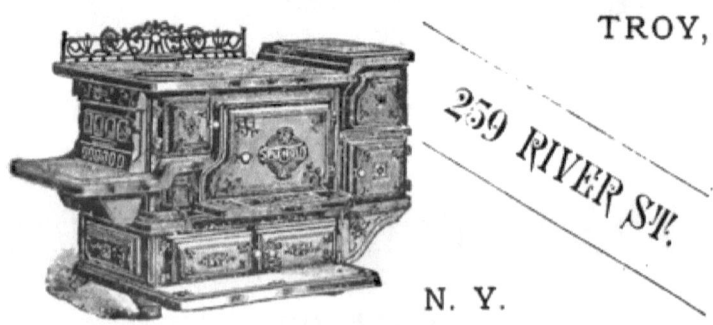

—DEALER IN—

FULLER & WARREN CO.'S
STOVES, HEATERS AND RANGES.

F. N. Salisbury & Co.

13 CONGRESS STREET,

TROY, N. Y.

Picture Frames

and Mouldings.

THE LARGEST STOCK AND THE CHEAPEST GOODS IN THE CITY.

WM. H. YOUNG,

BOOKSELLER, STATIONER

— : AND : —

Blank Book Manufacturer,

8 & 9 FIRST, AND 214 RIVER STS.,

TROY, N. Y.

Specialty made of Wedding and Visiting Cards.

246 RIVER STREET. FINEST STORE. **246 RIVER STREET.**

LARGEST STOCK. LOWEST PRICES.

Headquarters for Fine and Reliable Goods.

DIAMONDS, JEWELRY,
Fine American Watches,
Sterling Silver Novelties,
Clocks, Bronzes and Fancy Goods.

By far the largest stock and finest assortment of the above goods to be found North of New York City. You can depend upon getting reliable goods, and always the best in the market, as we do not sell cheap goods but give the best value for the money. QUICK SALES AND SMALL PROFITS is our motto, consequently our goods are continually moving, and always new and fresh.

SIM, THE TROY JEWELER.

246 RIVER STREET, *Opp. Steamboat Landing,* TROY, N. Y.

LARGEST REPAIRING DEPARTMENT IN TROY.
ONLY RELIABLE, SKILLED WORKMEN EMPLOYED.

SATISFACTION GUARANTEED OR MONEY CHEERFULLY REFUNDED.

AMERICAN WATCHES.
SAVE MONEY AND GET THE BEST IF YOU TRADE WITH **SIM**, THE POPULAR TROY JEWELER.

P. C. CURTIS, M. D.

Lake Avenue, cor. of Hedding Avenue,
ROUND LAKE, N. Y.

OFFICE HOURS: { 8 to 9 o'clock. A. M.
{ 1 to 2   "   P. M.
{ 7 to 8   "   "

CANDY & CONFECTIONS.

M. D. Saxe,

MANUFACTURER OF

Candy and Confections,

Nos. 303 & 305 River Street,
TROY, N. Y.

Retail Store:

No. 215 BROADWAY,   Between Second & Third Sts.

Sunday Schools, Fairs, and Societies furnished with Candy and Confections, at wholesale prices, in plain or ornamental boxes, cornucopias, and packages.

Christmas Tree Candles, Fixtures and Tinsels also supplied.

CONTRACTOR AND BUILDER.

W. H. ROSE,

BALLSTON SPA, N. Y.

BUILDER OF THE GEORGE WEST MUSEUM, GRIFFIN INSTITUTE, GARNSEY HALL AND OTHER BUILDINGS AT ROUND LAKE.

M. F. CUMMINGS,

Architect,

10 and 11 Times Building.

TROY, N. Y.

ARCHITECT OF THE GEORGE WEST MUSEUM, GRIFFIN INSTITUTE, GARNSEY HALL AND OTHER BUILDINGS AT ROUND LAKE.

(LIMITED) METROPOLITAN DRY GOODS STORES,

85 & 87 Third Street, and 57 & 59 Congress Street,

Third Street, Opposite City Hall,   Congress Street, Opposite Court House.

TROY, N. Y.

SAMPLES MAILED FREE UPON APPLICATION.

WOODLAWN.

This new and elegant House is located in one of the most desirable parts of the **ROUND LAKE GROUNDS**. It is large and substantial, and yet cosy and home-like.

It is first-class in all its appointments. The rooms are generous and well-ventilated. There are accommodations for one hundred guests.

The Proprietor has had several years' experience in hotel life, and will spare no pains for the comfort of his guests.

The **WOODLAWN** is located near the depot; not a half minute's walk. Baggage of patrons transferred to and from the depot free of charge.

WOODLAWN will be open for guests May 15th. Terms reasonable.

For information regarding Rooms, Board, &c., address

C. R. RULISON, Proprietor,
ROUND LAKE, N. Y.

New Crockery Store.

JESSUP & HENDERSON,

251 RIVER STREET,

(BURDETT BUILDING),

TROY, N. Y.

Breakfast, Dinner & Tea Sets,

GLASSWARE,

Chandeliers,
    Hanging, Bracket and Stand Lamps,
Table Cutlery,
    Ice Cream Freezers,
        Bird Cages.

THE CELEBRATED CROWN OIL STOVES.

No Old Stock.   All New Goods.

FIRST-CLASS WARES AT LOWEST PRICES.

With years of experience in this business in large wholesale and retail houses, we purchase our goods to sell at prices most favorable to all classes of purchasers.

Visit our spacious warerooms and see our wares.

251 RIVER STREET.

www.ingramcontent.com/pod-product-compliance
Lightning Source LLC
Chambersburg PA
CBHW030408170426
43202CB00010B/1535